CINCINNATI REDS
HALL OF
FAME
★★ *Highlights* ★★

GREG RHODES

CLERISY PRESS

CINCINNATI REDS
HALL OF
FAME
★★ *Highlights* ★★

FOR FURTHER INFORMATION, CONTACT THE PUBLISHER AT

CLERISY PRESS
1700 MADISON ROAD
CINCINNATI, OH 45206

Edited by
JACK HEFFRON

Cover and interior designed by
STEPHEN SULLIVAN

Photos courtesy of:
CINCINNATI REDS HALL OF FAME AND MUSEUM AND CINCINNATI REDS

Library of Congress Cataloging-in-Publication Data

Rhodes, Gregory L., 1946-
Cincinnati Reds Hall of Fame highlights / by Greg Rhodes.
p. cm.
ISBN-13: 978-1-57860-300-8 (alk. paper)
ISBN-10: 1-57860-300-5 (alk. paper)
1. Cincinnati Reds (Baseball team)--History. I. Title.

GV875.C65R46 2007
796.357'640977178--dc22

2007005406

Printed in the **USA**

TO THE

GREAT FANS

⇖ ℥ ⇕

THE

CINCINNATI REDS

ACKNOWLEDGMENTS

This book could not have been written without the support of the Cincinnati Reds Hall of Fame and Museum board and staff, and the Cincinnati Reds. Thanks to the Board of Directors of the Hall of Fame, including past-president Gary Gruber and current president Robert S. Castellini for supporting the project.

I want to personally thank Robert H. Castellini, the CEO of the Reds, for his support of the Reds Hall of Fame, and for writing the foreword to the book. Bob has a lifetime of Reds memories, and I appreciate his taking time to share some of his personal highlights for the introduction.

Thanks to the many members of the Reds staff for their assistance, including John Allen, COO, Karen Forgus, vice president of corporate affairs, Rob Butcher and the Reds media relations staff, and special thanks to Ralph Mitchell, Dann Stupp, and Jarrod Rollins of the creative services department for help with photo research.

I particularly want to thank my co-authors from previous Reds books. I referred to these books many times in the preparation of the Hall of Fame highlights, and their contributions to those earlier books are gratefully acknowledged. Thanks to John Snyder, my co-author on *Redleg Journal*, Mark Stang, my co-author on *Reds in Black and White*, and John Erardi, whom I partnered with on *First Boys of Summer, Crosley Field, Big Red Dynasty,* and *Opening Day.* Their contributions to this book are evident on nearly every page.

I also want to thank 700 WLW and the Reds on Radio Network, especially network coordinator Dave Armbruster, and network producer Russ Jackson. Both were instrumental in helping develop the concept for the show, in helping produce each segment, and in fine-tuning the scripts. Also thanks to Karrie Sudbrack, Darryl Parks, Lisa Braun, Joe Frederick, and Tom Horan at 700 WLW, and to Bill Bangert and Lance McAlister, hosts of the pre-game show in which the Hall of Fame highlights are heard.

Thanks to my colleagues here at the Cincinati Reds Hall of Fame—Chris Eckes, Brittney Morris, Craig Bradds, Gil Cedar, and our many floor staff and volunteers —for providing feedback on scripts and ideas for highlights.

Thanks to the staff of Clerisy Press: Richard Hunt for championing the idea, Jack Heffron for his outstanding editorial assistance, Steve Sullivan for his design of the cover and inside pages, and Howard Cohen for marketing and publicity.

CONTENTS

FOREWORD

by *Robert H. Castellini*, CEO, Cincinnati Reds

The history and tradition of the Reds help separate this ball club from all the others. A lot of teams have been around a long time, but I really believe no other club has the heritage we do. That's the reason we have the best team Hall of Fame and Museum in all of baseball. And that's why I am happy to write this foreword for this Reds Hall of Fame Highlights book; I know how much pride the fans have in their Reds.

For me, it started with our family trips to Crosley Field in the late 1940s. We had season tickets behind home plate, right under the screen. In those days, the screen went overhead and stretched all the way up to the upper deck. I still remember watching the foul balls hit the screen and then roll back down to the field, and of course I was hoping the ball would come off the side of the netting because then it would drop in the stands and we had a shot at catching it.

It was very much a family thing, going to the ballpark. My dad was always a big fan; he would entertain customers there. Mom was a big fan too. And my older sister was crazy about Frank McCormick, the big first baseman. You know, I can still remember the cigar smoke, the smell of cotton candy, the peanuts. Those were great times.

Of course everybody has a favorite player from growing up and watching the Reds. That period in the late 1940s, early 1950s, I remember watching Johnny Vander Meer—he was right at the end of his career. And Ewell "The Whip" Blackwell." He was unbelievable. Roy McMillan and Johnny Temple. And here's a couple of names you don't hear so much anymore: Grady Hatton and Andy Seminick. But Klu—Ted Kluszewski—he was the big guy. He was my favorite. There was just nobody like him.

One moment that stands out for me was in 1947, the first time Jackie Robinson came to Cincinnati with the Brooklyn Dodgers. People were talking about it in the stands, but when he came out for the first time, there was silence. Nobody said much. Then about the second inning, he made a nice play and everybody cheered. I didn't really understand at the time what it was about, but in retrospect it was quite a memorable moment.

I was building up our family business back in the 1970s when the Big Red Machine was at the top of the baseball world. And it was such a confidence builder for the whole city. There was such star-power on that team. National attention. It made us all very proud. Our company's reach was very similar to the Reds region—a circle reaching out two hundred miles from Cincinnati. We brought customers in all the time to see games at Riverfront. They would covet those tickets. Come in and see Rose and Bench and Morgan and Perez. The Big Red Machine. And then you had the excitement of the post-season. We went to every World Series game. I especially remember the Red Sox Series in 1975, because my in-laws were from Boston. That was something.

Before we bought the Reds in 2006, I was part of the St. Louis Cardinals ownership group. There were several of us from Cincinnati who had an interest in the club. I very much enjoyed that experience, but that was different from owning your hometown team! I wasn't living in St. Louis, so if the team was bad, I didn't have to be around. But now this is a whole different situation. This is my hometown club.

When Tom and Joe Williams and I first talked to Carl Lindner and George Strike about buying the Reds, we didn't have a partnership put together. But we knew who we wanted. We wanted people who cared about Cincinnati. We wanted hometown people They would be our best ambassadors for the club. And they would have that built-in pride. That's the kind of group we put together. And we knew if we could please them, then we would be pleasing the fans too.

Our job is to do the best for the people of Cincinnati and for the fans in Reds country. I know the expectations are high here. We are in a smaller city, but we have won five World Series and played in nine altogether. There's only a handful of clubs in baseball history that have done better. We bust our tails to be sure we have a contender and to be sure the fans have a great experience at the ballpark. It's a tough business. You have to put every last penny into it. You have to work smart.

The pride the city would have in another championship would make it all worthwhile. You are instilling in people, especially the kids, confidence and pride. "If the Reds can do it, so can I!" It picks up everybody. It gives everybody a "can-do" attitude.

To win more championships here, that is our goal. I was walking through our Hall of Fame one day and saw our World Series trophies on display. Greg Rhodes, our Hall of Fame director, told me he had room for one more. And I said, "One?! We're not stopping at one!"

I still root like I'm back at Crosley Field, a kid just sitting there loving the game. I'm still a fan at heart.

I know Reds fans will enjoy these highlight moments they've heard from Greg on the Reds Radio Network. There's a fascinating new story on every page. Did you know a group of young lawyers started the old Red Stockings? It's in the book.

INTRODUCTION

by *Greg Rhodes,* Executive Director, Reds Hall of Fame
Cincinnati Reds Team Historian

Prior to the 2005 season, shortly after the Cincinnati Reds Hall of Fame and Museum opened, Dave Armbruster, the producer of the Reds on Radio Network, talked to me about including a Reds history segment in the pre-game show that airs before each Reds game. We talked about a couple of different formats before deciding on a series of one-minute historical highlights that covered topics popular with Reds fans—with new information, or a twist on a familiar subject.

And there were plenty of good stories, although I must admit that by August, after having written over one hundred and twenty-five of the highlights, I was beginning to wonder if this was such a good idea!

By the end of the 2006 season, we had recorded some three hundred highlights. As I looked at the stack of scripts on my desk, I thought, "This could be a book!"

Fortunately, Clerisy Press agreed, and the *Cincinnati Reds Hall of Fame Highlights* book was born. We've arranged the pieces in chronological order to provide a clearer sense of the team's history, but you can pick up the book and start reading wherever you want. The highlights were originally written to be read aloud, so feel free to do so! You'll also find a lot of great photos of Reds heroes past and present, the guys who have given us so many wonderful memories.

If ever a club was worth of all this history, it is the Reds. And if ever a team and its fans deserved a hall of fame, it is the Reds franchise. The history of organized club baseball in Cincinnati dates back to the Civil War and the original professional team, the 1869 Red Stockings. The history of the club is on display in the museum year-round, and thousands of baseball fans have visited since the museum opened in the fall of 2004.

The Hall of Fame, as an honor for Reds players, dates to 1958. The first class of Reds Hall of Famers, elected by the fans, received their plaques at Crosley Field on the night of July 18. The original inductees? They were all stars of the 1939-40 championship era: pitchers Paul Derringer, Bucky Walters, and Johnny Vander Meer, first baseman Frank McCormick, and catcher Ernie Lombardi. Lombardi was later inducted into the National Baseball Hall of Fame in Cooperstown, New York. (And one could certainly make a strong case for Derringer and Walters, as well, but so far they have been overlooked by the voters.)

As of 2007, there are seventy-one members of the Reds Hall of Fame, making it the largest team hall of fame in baseball. We are also the oldest continuously operating team hall of fame.

The new museum, which houses the hall of fame plaques in an elegant gallery, has also quickly established itself as the premier team baseball museum, second only in reputation to the National Baseball Hall of Fame. Many fans who visit the our museum say, "This is better than Cooperstown!" Well, I am pleased to hear the compliments, although I respectfully disagree. After all, Cooperstown is the quintessential baseball museum. But I do think the fans are right in one respect. For a Reds fan, the Reds Hall of Fame probably is better than Cooperstown: an entire museum devoted to the story of their Cincinnati Reds, full of pictures and memorabilia that bring back many fond memories.

When I give presentations about the Reds Hall of Fame, I often say, "Parents, bring your kids; and kids, bring your parents." There are galleries for all ages in the Reds Hall of Fame. From the championships of 1919 and 1940 to the glory of the Big Red Machine and the joy of the 1990 "Wire-to-Wire" champs. From Roush and Rixey to Robinson and Rose. Baseball speaks to all generations, nuturing dreams and recalling memories.

I hope you recall a memory or two in these Reds Hall of Fame highlights.

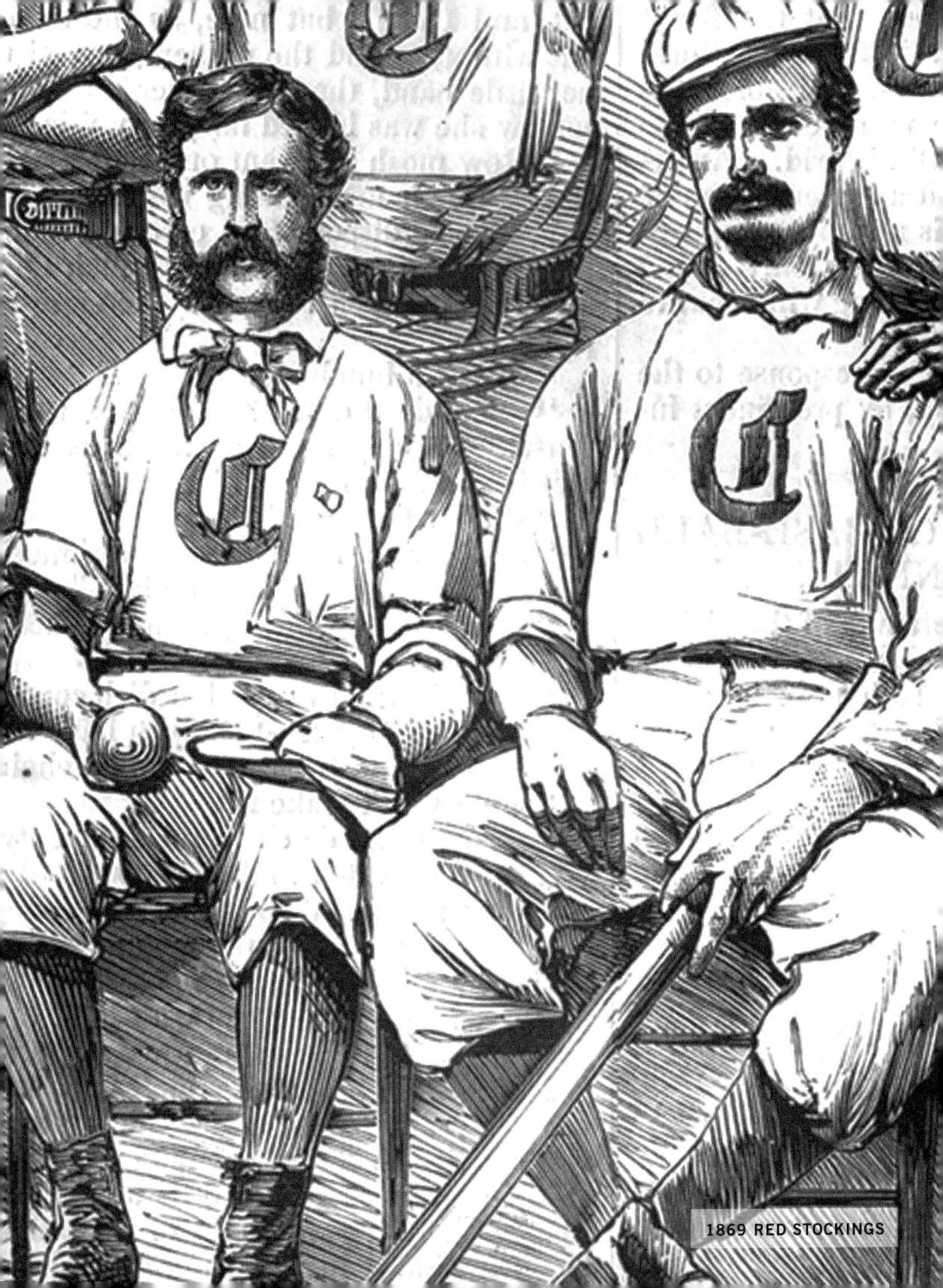

1869 RED STOCKINGS

RED STOCKINGS
AND WOODEN PARKS

1866-1879

IN THE BEGINNING

Cincinnati fans love their old Red Stockings, baseball's first professional team, the namesake of today's Reds. Baseball history in this city dates all the way back to that team of 1869, when the club decided to pay each and every player a salary. But in fact, the baseball club that sponsored the Red Stockings had existed before that year. It was just an amateur club and was one of many such teams in the Queen City that sprang up after the Civil War. The club was formed in the summer of 1866 by a group of attorneys who wanted to play this new sport of baseball. They named the club the "Resolutes," but later changed the name to the Cincinnati Base Ball Club—which does sound a little more lawerly. They hired Harry Wright to manage the team. At that time this meant Harry

THE 1869 CINCINNATI RED STOCKINGS, THE FIRST PROFESSIONAL BASEBALL TEAM.

was the captain...and the grounds crew...and the scorekeeper...and the pitcher! The 1866 team played only four matches. The next year they attracted some of the best players in the city, went seventeen and one, and established themselves as the top club in Cincinnati. Two years later, club officials decided they wanted to challenge the best teams in the East for supremacy in baseball. The way to do it? Attract better players. And how to do it? Pay 'em. And so, the professional revolution began, all from the humble beginnings of the "Resolutes" in 1866.

THIS TEAM PHOTO OF THE 1869 CINCINNATI RED STOCKINGS WAS TAKEN IN WASHINGTON D.C. BY THE FAMOUS PHOTOGRAPHER MATTHEW BRADY. (BACK ROW, L-R) CAL MCVEY, CHARLIE GOULD, HARRY WRIGHT, GEORGE WRIGHT, FRED WATERMAN. (FRONT ROW, L-R) ANDY LEONARD, DOUG ALLISON, ASA BRAINARD, CHARLIE SWEASY.

THE PRO REVOLUTION

In 1869 the Cincinnati Base Ball Club decided to offer players a contract with guaranteed salaries over the season. Before this decision, some players had been paid, but it was always under the table and was usually based on a percentage of gate receipts. But the Cincinnati system was different. The players were now actually employees of the club, guaranteed a check. The payroll of that first Red Stocking team was a whopping eleven thousand dollars, with the star players making close to two grand. To put that number in perspective, at the time the mayor of Cincinnati was making four thousand dollars. A school principal? About twenty-five hundred dollars. Back in those days, if you wanted the big bucks, you were better off being a principal than a baseball player.

NO TAFT IN THE LINEUP

Did you ever hear the story that Ty Cobb, the rough-and-tumble Hall of Fame outfielder, killed someone during his career? Well, it turns out, Cobb got in more than his share of fights, but he never murdered anybody. And there's another rumor you sometimes hear about our Cincinnati native William Howard Taft, the twenty-sixth president of the United States. Seems that Taft once played for the 1869 Cincinnati Red Stockings. Or so the story goes. But if you do just a little bit of research, it turns out Taft was all of twelve years old in 1869, and he never played for the Reds. It is true that Taft once said he would rather have been president of the Cincinnati Base Ball Club than president of the United States. At least he had his priorities straight.

CARRIAGES ON THE FIELD

Imagine for a moment you are back in the old wooden grandstands watching the famous 1869 Red Stockings. You would certainly recognize the game as baseball:

nine players on a side, three outs per inning. But wait, there's something odd: carriages parked in the outfield! Back then, most people walked to the game or rode the streetcars. But people of the upper classes might drive their own carriage to the ball game. Since there were no parking lots, where would you put it? You didn't want to risk leaving it unattended outside the park, so the club provided a wide "carriage" gate in the fence so that carriages could be parked in foul territory inside the ballpark. But when the crowds were big, the line of carriages would stretch all the way into fair ground up against the outfield fence, and your vehicle and horse were in play. If a ball rolled under them, the fielders had to crawl around and find it! Now there's a sight you're not likely to see today, that's for sure.

ENTERPRISING CONDUCTORS STAND IN FRONT OF A HORSE-DRAWN STREETCAR,
WHICH TOOK PEOPLE TO THE GAMES AT UNION GROUNDS. THE SIGN ATOP THE
STREETCAR ADVERTISES THE DAY'S GAME.

A SAD DAY IN BROOKLYN

Eighteen seventy marked the final season of the historic professional Cincinnati Red Stockings, the forerunner of today's Reds. The Red Stockings had become the first all-professional team in 1869, and the starting nine was re-signed for the 1870 season at salaries averaging about a thousand dollars a year. The popularity of the famous Red Stockings was so widespread, the club was invited to New Orleans to play a series of games, and they headed south on a two-week tour in late April. They didn't call it spring training, but in effect that's what it was, although the games were considered official and not exhibitions. The club continued its winning ways—it had won fifty-seven games in a row in 1869—and the winning streak reached eighty-one when the Red Stockings took the field against the Brooklyn Atlantics in Brooklyn on June 14. The game was tied after nine innings, and in the rules of the day, the Red Stockings could have accepted the tie. But team captain Harry Wright did not want this blemish on the record, and so the teams played on into the eleventh inning. The Red Stockings tallied twice, but Brooklyn responded with three runs, and the fabulous winning streak came to an end. The Red Stockings went on to lose five more times in 1870, but their two-year record of 124-6 remains an unbelievable accomplishment.

GOING BROKE

Escalating payrolls, rising ticket prices. Sounds all too familiar to modern fans, who often long for the days when the business of baseball didn't make the front page. But financial problems are as old as the professional game itself, and you only have your Cincinnati Red Stockings to blame. That original pro club in 1869 showed a profit of just a dollar and thirty-nine cents after its first season, and in 1870, the club raised ticket prices, from twenty-five cents to fifty cents, hoping to improve its financial condition, but to no avail. By the end of the 1870 season, the club's finances were as red as the team's socks. The players were beginning to get offers from other clubs for more money. The team officials met and decided it call it quits. "You can talk about the glory of the Red Stockings, but you can't run the club on glory," said one official. "Baseball doesn't pay as it used to." Let me repeat that statement: "Baseball doesn't pay as it used to." That said in 1870! And so the city that founded the professional game gave it up after just two years. For the next five seasons, professional baseball continued in cities around America, but not in Cincinnati, where it had all begun.

THE MISSING YEARS

The phenomenal success of the Cincinnati Red Stockings in 1869 and '70 clearly proved that the professional game was superior to the amateur one. After financial problems forced the club to give up professional play after the 1870 season, it

CHARLIE GOULD

wasn't until the Reds joined the new National League in 1876 that big-time baseball returned to Cincinnati. But what happened in those missing years, 1871-1875? As it turns out, baseball didn't just disappear. Dozens of amateur clubs still played regularly, and in 1875, one of the founders of the original Red Stockings team re-organized a professional nine. He even hired one of the old Red Stockings, first baseman Charlie Gould, to captain the team. They played exhibition games against the top clubs in the country and drew capacity crowds at their temporary field across the Ohio River in nearby Ludlow, Kentucky. In September of 1875, the club opened a new ballpark by the stockyards along Spring Grove Avenue, about four miles north of downtown, and the next spring this Reds team joined seven other clubs to form the National League.

THE 1870 RED STOCKINGS POSE WITH THEIR CLEVELAND RIVALS, THE FOREST CITYS,
ON MAY 31 IN CLEVELAND. THIS IS THE ONLY KNOWN PHOTOGRAPH OF THE
RED STOCKINGS APPEARING ON A PLAYING FIELD.

A NEW LEAGUE

It's 1876, and teams in eight cities come together to form the new National League. Joining Cincinnati in this venture were the now familiar major league cities of Boston, Chicago, New York, Philadelphia, and St. Louis, plus Louisville and Hartford. Opening Day was April 25, just six weeks after Alexander Graham Bell invented the telephone. Good thing Bell didn't try to call the Reds. There was nobody home. The Reds were awful in 1876. They wound up with the worst record in club history, 9-56, and drew all of twenty-four thousand fans to their thirty home games, an average of just eight hundred fans a game. They were probably lucky to have that many show up.

YOUR "CUTE" REDS

In 1877, organized major league baseball was still in its infancy. When the National League formed the year before, the teams were only scheduled to play sixty games. And for the first time ever, there was actually a pre-arranged schedule. The dates for all games were announced and schedules were printed, but the Cincinnati fans were not exactly knocking the doors down to the ballpark. In twenty-nine home games in 1877, the Reds drew only a thousand fans a game. Of course, when you have a 15-42 record and finish last, it isn't likely you are going to draw very well. The Reds were terrible in those early years. You could say they were broke, and that was literally true. Halfway through the season, the club went bankrupt. Without any cash on hand, the team simply quit playing games for three weeks until they found a new owner. One of the first acts of new ownership was to dress up the players with different colored hats. The players wore red, white, blue, and green caps, some with stripes. The paper reported that the players looked "cute." But they still couldn't win.

HISTORY-MAKING MOMENTS

After 135 years of records and statistics, it is rare to see a baseball "first." But all these records had to start sometime, and, not surprisingly, the early days of baseball saw many historic milestones. On September 6, 1877, in just the second year of the National League, the Reds had three history-making moments in the same game! The Reds defeated Louisville in Cincinnati, 1-0, behind the pitching of southpaw Bobby Mitchell. Mitchell made history by being the first left-handed pitcher ever to appear in a game. The shutout was the first ever in club history, and during the game, Reds outfielder Lip Pike (who just happened to be the first Jewish professional player), hit the first over-the-fence home run in Reds history. What a day!

LIP PIKE

GLOVES AND BUTTERCUPS

The Reds played over .600 ball in 1878 and finished second in the National League. But a quick look at that season reveals just how new the game of baseball was, and how much it was different from today's game. First thing you notice is they only played sixty games. The season didn't start until May 1, and the clubs averaged about three games a week. The schedule may account for the fact that the Reds used just two pitchers! They used just eleven players in all in 1878. They had one regular substitute whose name was…"Buttercup." "Buttercup" Dickerson. It is without doubt one of the all-time great nicknames in Reds lore. The Cincinnati catcher also made a historic debut, becoming the first Reds catcher to wear a mask. And if you were reading the baseball guides of the era, you came across an unusual ad, featuring a large padded object that was called a "catcher's glove." It was the first time an ad for gloves had appeared in the *Spalding Guide*.

FRISKY REDLEGS

Eighteen seventy-nine marked a couple of notable milestones. In New Jersey, Thomas Edison developed the modern light bulb, and in Cincinnati, Proctor and Gamble produced a new soap called Ivory. But at the ballpark, near the stockyards off Spring Grove Avenue, the Reds of 1879 did absolutely nothing of note, finishing fifth in the eight-team league. Those Reds were picked to do better. Some had predicted the Reds to win the pennant. But when the team got off to a disappointing start, the local press blew the whistle on the club. Seems some of the boys were a little out of control. And the press was hardly subtle in its criticism: A few of the players are "sacrificing themselves for the sake of a little wine or beer. It is no secret to the public, and might as well be put down in black and white, that one or two and maybe as many as four, of the Cincinnati players have been drinking too liberally, and bumming around too injudiciously....Some of the unmarried men ought to be gathered up and corralled somewhere." Well, boys will be boys, even in 1879.

WILL WINS THEM ALL

Here's a record that falls into the "it will never be broken" category, a record that is really so amazing it is hard to believe it truly exists. That is the mark of seventy-five complete games in one season. It's the major league record, and it's held by the Reds Will White, who pitched in the 1870s and '80s. There were a few things different about pitching back then that allowed a record like this to happen. Pitching was underhand, and the mound was set at forty-five feet. The strain on the arm wasn't so great. Teams usually carried just two pitchers. And one pitcher could start and finish nearly every game if he was good enough. And White was. Great, in fact. His record was set in 1879. He won forty-three of his seventy-five complete games. In fact he pitched in every game the Reds won that year.

THOUGH HE LOOKED MORE LIKE A CLERK THAN A MAJOR LEAGUER, WILL WHITE WAS ONE OF THE MOST DOMINATING PITCHERS OF HIS ERA.

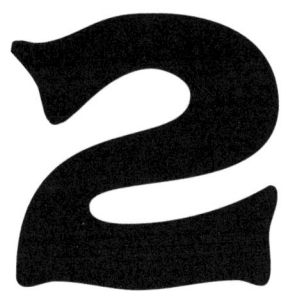

TWO LEAGUES

1880-1899

BENEFIT PACKAGE

In 1880, things were a little different from today. The season didn't begin until May 1, the schedule only called for eighty games, the players didn't wear gloves, pitching was underhand from forty-five feet, there was no mound, and the Reds played in a little wooden park a few blocks north of where they would eventually play in Crosley Field. Nothing much to report on that 1880 season. The Reds finished dead last. Do you think their team batting average of .224 might have had something to do with that? Today if you hit .224 you're going to be sent back to the minors. But that's what the whole team averaged in 1880. Here's another story from that season to illustrate how different conditions were. In a game on May 13, with the Reds hosting Cleveland, two of the Cleveland outfielders collided chasing a ball, and one broke his leg. At that time, players who were unable to play for an extended time were dropped from the payroll. If you couldn't play, no matter what the reason, no check. But his teammates were sympathetic. Four days later, on an off-day, Cleveland and Cincinnati scheduled an exhibition game for the benefit of the injured player and raised five hundred dollars.

MAN OVERBOARD!

John Reilly of Cincinnati had an excellent ten-year career with his hometown Reds, between 1880 and 1891, but Reilly, whose six-foot, three-inch frame earned him the nickname "Long John," almost didn't survive his rookie season. Literally. On a road trip to the Northeast in June of 1880, the Reds had a couple of off-days, and

Reilly went sightseeing in New York City. He took a steamboat on his return to the club, and near midnight, in dense fog, his boat collided with another boat and began to sink. Reilly helped the crew launch lifeboats and tried to rescue passengers. But with the boat sinking, Reilly jumped overboard and began paddling. The current proved too strong, and he drifted away from the rescue boats. Luckily he was discovered by a nearby vessel and finally rescued. However, he was reported missing by the papers, and his teammates were mourning his loss the next time they took the field. But Reilly was finally able to get word out that news of his death had been greatly exaggerated, and he returned to the Reds a few days later.

"LONG" JOHN REILLY TOWERS OVER TEAMMATE
HUGH NICOL, ONE OF THE SHORTEST MEN EVER TO
PLAY IN THE MAJOR LEAGUES.

NO BEER? NO GAMES!

In 1881 the Reds finished...well, they didn't finish. They didn't even start! It's the only year since the Reds joined the National League in 1876 that there was no professional Reds team in Cincinnati. New rules forced the Reds to close up shop for the season. Here's what happened: The NL adopted rules for 1881 that included a ban on the clubs renting their parks for use on Sunday. There were no league games scheduled on Sunday, but the Reds wanted to pull in extra income by renting their field to local amateur and semi-pro teams for Sunday play. The Reds might have agreed to this arrangement, if it weren't for the second new rule change: the clubs were banned from selling alcoholic beverages at the ballpark. No beer at the ballpark? How could the good citizens of Cincinnati enjoy a game at the park without a sip or two? The Reds, who had struggled financially in 1880, decided they could not make ends meet with these new rules, and so the owners pulled out of the league. There was no pro baseball in Cincinnati in 1881, but the Reds joined with five other clubs to form a new league, the American Association, in 1882 and return baseball...with beer...to the Queen City, where it has flourished ever since.

YOUR DAPPER REDS

Let's go back to 1882. This was the first season the Reds won a pennant, although you might wonder how. They were led by a rookie second baseman who played barehanded, a left-handed third baseman, and the first pitcher to wear glasses. At one point the players all wore different colored jerseys that were supposed to help fans identify them. I guess nobody thought of numbers. The pitcher wore a brown shirt, the catcher dark red, the first baseman red and white stripes, and so on. The club dropped the idea after a few games. Late in the season, the club faced a serious discipline problem. One of their players quit the team after he was fined five dollars—for making a one-handed catch! But the Reds didn't let any of this bother them that season. The schedule called for only eighty games, and the Reds won fifty-five of them, which would translate to 111 wins in today's schedule.

THE 1882 CHAMPION REDS LOOKED DAPPER, IF A LITTLE STRANGE, IN THEIR
MULTI-COLORED UNIFORMS. (BOTTOM ROW, L-R) JIMMY MACULLAR, HARRY WHEELER.
(MIDDLE ROW, L-R) HICK CARPENTER, POP SNYDER, WILL WHITE, CHUCK FULLMER,
JOE SOMMER. (TOP ROW, L-R) HARRY McCORMICK, "GRANDMOTHER" POWERS,
ECKY STEARNS, BID McPHEE

HOME RUN PARADISE

In 1883, the Reds were the defending champions of the American Association, and
they were almost successful in repeating as champs but finished five games out of
first. That 1883 team had something in common with today's Reds and Great American Ball Park. They played in a park called Bank Street Grounds, and in 1883, for
some unexplained reason, the park became a home run paradise, much like GABP is
today. There were more home runs hit at the old Bank Street ballpark than any other
park in the league. Now, the totals were pitifully small compared to today. In 2006,
there were 241 home runs hit at Great American Ball Park; in 1883, there were
forty-two home runs hit at the Reds park—but that was enough to rank number one.
John Reilly, who led the team in home runs that year with all of ten, became the first
player in Reds history to hit two home runs in one game. Shades of Babe Ruth!

TRIALS AND TRIBULATIONS

Eighteen eighty-four was one of those years in Cincinnati history when the fortunes of the Reds took a backseat to events of much greater significance. In February, the worst flood in the city's history to that time spread destruction up and down the Ohio River and throughout the low-lying areas of Cincinnati. The city had not recovered from the flood when a month later a major riot broke out downtown, centering on the courthouse. Mobs of citizens protested what they perceived to be lenient treatment of a murder suspect, and they set fire to the courthouse. The rioting lasted for two days with police under attack and shooting back at the mob to restore order. Some fifty-six people lost their lives. To this day, it is the worst civic disorder the city has ever experienced. Somehow, despite all this mayhem, the baseball club managed to build a new wooden ballpark, at the corner of Findlay and Western Avenue in the West End. Given all the other troubles in the city, it is perhaps not surprising to learn that a section of the stands collapsed on Opening Day, injuring over a dozen spectators. Despite the inauspicious start, the site proved to be very popular. Over the years a number of ballparks were built on this site, including historic Crosley Field.

TIMMMMBER!

The Reds opened a new wooden grandstand on Opening Day in 1884. Playing in the American Assocation, they opened against a team from Columbus. It was a cold, damp day, and a sloppy game that featured fifteen errors. The Reds lost, 10-9. But the real drama was just beginning. As the fans crowded onto a wooden platform at the rear of the stands, a support beam snapped and about fifty spectators tumbled twelve feet to the ground. There were cuts, bruises, and some broken bones. The Reds sent the team doctor to tend to the injured and ran ads in the paper to assure fans that the rest of the grandstand was safe. You know it was a different era back then because not one lawsuit was filed against the club.

MAKING THE NEWS

A number of unusual events took place in 1885, including the first appearance of overhand pitching in Cincinnati. The league made it legal that year, and fans were treated to the site of pitchers throwing from above the shoulder for the first time. At least legally—the rule change was implemented in part because pitchers kept cheating on their deliveries under the old rules. League officials finally gave up on restricting the pitchers' delivery and let the boys throw from whatever angle they wanted. Another interesting sight for Reds fans in 1885 was the appearance of O.P. Caylor as manager of the club. Now, Caylor was no ordinary manager. He was never a player, nor much of an athlete. In fact, he was a newspaper reporter who covered the Reds. This must have been a fantasy come true! Most of us think we could manage a ball club. Just give us a chance. Actually, Caylor wasn't too bad. He ran the club for two years and finished with a winning record. His 1885 Reds finished in second place with a fine record of 63-49, earning him a second season. But his 1886 Reds slumped to fifth, and Caylor was let go, perhaps earning him a front-page story the hard way.

THE 1885 REDS

THIS RARE ACTION PHOTO OF THE REDS PLAYING
AT LEAGUE PARK WAS TAKEN SOMETIME
BETWEEN 1884 AND 1893.

COMPLETE GAME, THE HARD WAY

Eighteen eighty-six was the year one of baseball's most important publications began, The *Sporting News,* out of St. Louis. For many years its comprehensive coverage of the game earned it the nickname "The Bible of Baseball." In 1886 it is fair to say it didn't spill a lot of ink on the Reds, who finished fifth, twenty-seven games out of first. One Reds pitcher was glad he didn't draw a lot of attention. On April 27, George Pechiney pitched a complete game for the Reds, which was typical for the time. But what was unusual was that the Reds lost, 20-2. Pechiney gave up all twenty runs, and the Reds never sent in a reliever. Gee, what did they have against the guy? But the worst performance of the year was saved for the Cincinnati fans, who on July 11 staged a riot at the ballpark. A fistfight erupted in the stands, which turned into a brawl, and other fans took the opportunity to throw beer glasses at the umpire who had ruled against the Reds on a couple of close plays. Order was finally restored after the umpire took refuge in the owners box, and several players grabbed bats to threaten the unruly crowd. Ah, nothing like a day at the ballpark...

YOUR RED-LEGGED PORKOPOLITANS

Over the years the Cincinnati club has had a number of team nicknames. Of course, the first was Red Stockings, which was popular until the press and the fans shortened it to Reds. In the 1950s, the team took on the name Redlegs, which is still occasionally used. But a few other names have come and gone. What about the Pioneers? The club trotted out that idea in 1886 to honor the team's legacy as the founders of professional baseball, but the name never caught on. One reason the club tried out Pioneers was it had grown tired of another nickname the press had been using: the Porkopolitans, a reference to the city's reputation as a meat-packing center. Your Cincinnati Porkopolitans. It would have been interesting to see what that team logo might have looked like!

AND THE COUNT IS FOUR AND THREE

In 1887, the Reds were led by their Hall of Fame second baseman, Bid McPhee, and the club finished second, playing .600 ball. I am always reminded when looking back at the game in this era just how different it was. We often think of baseball as a timeless game, unchanged over the decades, but in fact, even the basic rules of baseball have changed. Three strikes and four balls for example. It's always been that way, right? Well, no. In 1887, the rule was four strikes and five balls; a full count would have been four and three. Pitching was from fifty feet, not the modern distance of sixty feet, six inches. Today, the Reds or any team would die to have two twenty-game winners. In 1887, the Reds had two **thirty**-game winners. Veteran

BID McPHEE

Tony Mullane won thirty-one games, and nineteen-year-old rookie Elmer Smith won thirty-four and led the league in ERA. Elmer certainly would have won the Rookie of the Year Award if it had existed. Smith was something of an early Babe Ruth. He had an outstanding pitching record, but switched to the outfield at the age of twenty-four and wound up with a career batting average of .310. By the way, the modern rule of four balls and three strikes? It was established in 1889.

THE HOME OPENER...IN KANSAS CITY?

The year was 1888, and the Reds finished fourth, eleven games out of first, but it was the opening of the season we remember more than the finish. For this was the one and only year the Reds have ever been scheduled to open on the road. Although Cincinnati had opened every year at home prior to this one, the tradition of the home opener was not yet written in stone, and in 1888 the schedule makers sent Cincinnati to open in Kansas City. The Reds also stopped in St. Louis and Louisville on this western road trip before finally playing their first home game on May 1. The year 1888 proved to be memorable in baseball for one other reason. In June, a San Francisco newspaper published a baseball poem called "Casey at the Bat." "And somewhere men are laughing, and little children shout," ...running through the galleries at the Reds Hall of Fame, no doubt.

ERRORS GALORE

In 1889, the Reds had a decent team, finishing fourth in the eight-team league. All in all, in the 1880s, the Reds had a very good record, finishing above .500 all but one year. When you look back at this decade, a couple of things jump out. This was an offensive period in baseball, even more than today's power-laden game. Today's National League clubs average about 4.5 runs per game. But in 1889, teams were scoring over six runs a game. Yet the pitchers' ERAs were in the mid-threes, which would suggest a problem with catching the ball. And sure enough, check out that errors column. Teams made three to four times as many errors as they do today. The Reds shortstop in 1889 made **eighty-seven** errors, enough for an entire team today. Of course they practically played barehanded, using only very primitive gloves, so I guess we should give them a break. Another big difference from today is the nicknames: the Reds of 1889 featured "The Little Globetrotter" behind the plate, "The Count" and "Cyclone Jim" on the mound, "Long John" at first base, "White Wings" and "Bug" in the outfield, and "Bid" and "Hick" in the infield.

THE 1889 REDS—SLICK DRESSERS BUT NOT SUCH SLICK FIELDERS. THE MAN IN THE MIDDLE IS TEAM PRESIDENT AARON STERN. FROM TOP ROW, L-R: JAMES KEENAN, LEON VIAU, ELMER SMITH, TONY MULLANE, HICK CARPENTER, BUG HOLLIDAY, WHITE WINGS TEBEAU, HUGH NICOL, KID BALDWIN, BID McPHEE, LONG JOHN REILLY, OLLIE BEARD, MANAGER GUS SCHMELZ, TREASURER LOUIS HAUCK.

THREE OWNERS, THREE LEAGUES

The Reds and the National League: a combination as familiar as bread and butter, as mom and apple pie. But it wasn't always so. In the 1880s, the Reds played in a second major league called the American Association. But after the 1889 season, a new owner bought the club and announced he would put the Reds in a brand new league called the Player's Association. But the new league folded before it ever got off the ground, and the Reds said they would stay in the American Association. But wait: a new owner bought the club and announced he would move the team to the National League, where the Reds have been ever since. But what a crazy off-season. Three different owners, each wanting to put the Reds in a different league. And you thought the shenanigans of modern baseball were confusing!

401 INNINGS!

The year is 1890, and the Reds are back playing in the NL after nine seasons in the American Association. Home sweet home. They spent thirty-six days in first place and led by four and a half games on July 4. That club featured future Hall of Famer Bid McPhee and a rookie pitcher who would have been another Rookie of the Year if they had such a thing back then. Twenty-one-year-old Billy Rhines won twenty-eight games, had an ERA of 1.95 and pitched 401...I said 401...innings! But the wheels fell off in the second half, and the Reds wound up fourth. One other thing the fans loved that 1890 season. To protect the spectators sitting behind home plate, the club tried out a new idea: a wire screen to block foul balls. What will they think of next?

BILLY RHINES, KNOWN FOR HIS RUBBER ARM AND SUBMARINE DELIVERY, TWICE LED THE LEAGUE IN ERA.

A PARADE FOR THE OPENER

In 1891, the Reds played in a small ballpark in the West End of Cincinnati on the same site where Crosley Field would eventually stand. But in 1891, it was called League Park, and it was built entirely of wood and perhaps seated as many six thousand. Most of the seats were uncovered, and on a summer day, you might have taken your umbrella or "parasol," as it was then called, to provide some shade from the hot sun. Of course, most days you didn't have to worry about buying a ticket. The club averaged all of fourteen hundred fans for their home games. I'm telling you all the details about the ballpark because frankly, there's not much to say about the 1891 season. The Reds, who were called the worst-disciplined team in the league by a pre-season baseball publication, certainly played like it, finishing in seventh place, thirty games out of first. The 1891 highlight might have come on Opening Day when the Reds staged the first Opening Day Parade in Cincinnati, which consisted of three streetcars, one with the Reds, one with their opponents, and one carrying a band, rolling through downtown and winding up at the ballpark.

SPLIT SEASONS

In 1892, and for the first time in history, the season was played with a split-season schedule. The National League had added four new teams for a total of twelve, and the baseball owners decided to split the season in two with the first-half pennant race ending on July 15. The Reds finished fourth in the first-half race and eighth in the second half, and wound up fifth overall. The split-season format was scrapped after just this one year, and the only other time it has happened was in 1981 when the owners tried it after a strike interrupted the season. There are a couple of interesting sidelights from that 1892 season. For the first time while members of the National League, the Reds played a game on Sunday. Prior to 1892, the league wouldn't allow it. And on the final day of the season, a young Reds rookie pitcher named Bumpus Jones started his first game in the big leagues…and threw a no-hitter! He made the starting lineup the next season, but hurt his arm and wound up winning only two games in his entire career. But half his wins were no-hitters.

TOO MUCH SUNSHINE

Here's a headline that would catch your attention: Today's game called on account of…sunshine! As ridiculous as that sounds, this actually happened to the Reds one sunny day in 1892. Their old ballpark, which stood on the site of the future Crosley Field, was built facing west. The batter looked directly into the sun in the late afternoon, and the hitters and catchers often complained they couldn't see the ball. One afternoon as the sun slowly sank in the west, it seemed to stop just above Price Hill. The umpire called a brief delay, and then announced he was stopping the game. He declared the conditions were too dangerous. Why they couldn't have waited just a few more minutes is beyond me, but even the paper called the decision a "just and sensible one." So, forget about rain. Do you think fans had to ask, "What are the chances of sun today?"

HOLLIDAYS AND WEDDINGS

The Reds finished sixth, in the middle of the pack of the twelve-team National League, in 1893, and, while they didn't have much offense that year, they did set a club record by scoring **thirty** runs in one game against Louisville. One of the hitting stars that day was Bug Holliday, who hit two home runs, including a grand slam. Holliday, an outfielder, was on a path that could have put him in Cooperstown. His offensive numbers were excellent; he twice led the league in home runs. But at the age of twenty-eight he suffered an appendicitis attack, and for some reason he did not fully recover. He was never again a full-time player. The other big story in 1893 involved a groundskeeper, not a player. The Reds assistant groundskeeper, Louis Can, married Rosie Smith at home plate prior to a game on September 18, and the heavily promoted event drew the largest Monday crowd of the season—2,201 attended, including a large group of "ladies," according to the paper. The Cincinnati players raised sixty dollars in cash for the couple, and even the visiting Baltimore club pitched in another forty dollars. The couple drew considerable attention for the stunt, and the paper reported a few days later that they had received offers to appear at circus-like events. A year later, the couple had a son and wanted to have him baptized at home plate, but the Reds politely declined.

ASSISTANT GROUNDSKEEPER LOUIS CAN MARRIES ROSIE SMITH IN LEAGUE PARK
AT HOME PLATE.

NEW STANDS, BUT TENTH PLACE

In 1894, the Reds finished in tenth place. There were twelve teams in the National League back then, and no divisions, so all twelve competed in one big league. The tenth-place finish was the lowest the Reds ever had. The season had begun with high hopes, however. The Reds opened a new grandstand that year called League Park. It stood at the corner of Findlay and Western, on the same site Crosley Field would occupy years later. The architects elevated the grandstand so it would be out of the flood plain of the Mill Creek, creating a big space under the grandstand. The club sold cheap standing-room tickets, and the area began to be called Rooter's Row. Sometimes the Rooters rooted a little too boisterously and the next season, the Reds strung barbed wire in front of Rooter's Row to keep the cranks, as the fans were then called, from going out onto the field. Nothing like baseball in Cincinnati.

THE LAWN MOWERS WANDERED OFF

There is nothing quite as pleasing to the eye as walking into Great American Ball Park and seeing that lush green grass of the baseball field. It can take your breath away—perfectly trimmed, the alternating light and dark shades in the grass that trace the mower's path. As you can imagine, the field is well cared for with the grounds crew working on it daily, trimming and watering and fertilizing. But imagine for a minute the fields in baseball's early years. The game has been around a lot longer than power mowers or sophisticated watering systems. How did they manage those fields in the 1800s? Well, here's a clue from the Cincinnati newspaper of July 1894. Seems the head groundskeeper was on the lookout for a few sheep that disappeared from the ballpark. The sheep were kept around to help naturally trim the long grass, and groundskeeper Matty Schwab, like Little Bo Peep, had lost his sheep. They were finally discovered a couple of days later across town. Well, at least today, the grounds crew doesn't have to worry about their lawn mowers running away.

PACKIN' 'EM IN

Back in 1895, the Reds wound up eighth in the twelve-team league, so the fans didn't have much to cheer about. But one game was a huge sell-out. About eleven thousand spectators filled the Cincinnati park on May 19 to watch the Reds play Washington. The sell-out was due in part to the hundreds of fans who traveled on excursion trains from Columbus to see their hometown boy, Kip Selbach, pitch for the Senators. And as it turned out, a few too many fans showed up. In the seventh inning, the sun worshippers sitting in the wooden bleachers in right field suddenly heard a loud crack, and a portion of the bleachers crashed to the ground. It fell an estimated fifteen feet, but only three injuries were reported. Despite the confusion, order was restored in about ten minutes, with most of the now seatless fans finding space in the outfield grass to sit and watch the rest of the game. Now, those were loyal fans.

FIRST PITCH

Throwing out a ceremonial first pitch is standard practice at most games. The first time it happened in Cincinnati was way back on Opening Day of 1895, when Mayor John Caldwell, sitting in the front

1895 REDS FROM THE *SPALDING GUIDE*

row of the stands, simply handed a new ball to the umpire to launch the season. Opening Day was apparently the only time during the season when a first pitch ceremony was held. The first time the ball was thrown from the mound instead of the stands was in 1913 by Mayor Henry Hunt. For the record, his toss was high and outside. Perhaps the most historic first pitch came on Opening Day 2006, when President George Bush became the first sitting president to throw out a first pitch on Opening Day in Cincinnati. The ball is on display at the Reds Hall of Fame, joining another Bush ball, one from George H. W. Bush, who helped inaugurate Great American Ball Park by throwing out the first pitch on Opening Day, 2003.

THE TEMPLE CUP

In the late 1890s, the Reds consistently had very good teams. They always finished above .500. Twice they topped .600, including the 1896 season, when they finished third with a winning percentage of .606, which would translate to ninety-eight wins in today's schedule. Those clubs remind me somewhat of the teams of the late 1980s. Both were managed by great ballplayers who had grown up in southwest Ohio. The Reds of the late 1980s were managed by Pete Rose, of course, and in the late 1890s they were led by Buck Ewing, the Cooperstown Hall of Famer, who was born near Hillsboro. Despite having contenders every year, neither Rose's nor Ewing's Reds ever won a pennant. Ewing's teams played in an era before there was a World Series, but in 1896 the league did sponsor a championship playoff of sorts, called the Temple Cup, a playoff between the first- and second-place teams in the National League. And the Reds were in contention until a late-season slump. With the playoff spot on the line, the Reds dropped two of three to Cleveland at the end of the season and finished two and one-half games out of the playoffs.

BAREHANDED BID

Imagine playing baseball barehanded. The sting of the ball, the bruises sure to result. But this is exactly what old-time players did in the early years of baseball before gloves became popular in the 1880s. By the mid-1890s, every player but one was wearing a glove. The lone holdout? It was the Reds second baseman, Bid

McPhee. McPhee began his major league career in 1882 and had played without a glove. He couldn't understand why players were using them. "This glove business has gone a little too far," McPhee said. "True, hot-hit balls do sting, but after you get used to it, there is no trouble on that score." But, McPhee finally gave in and put on the leather in 1896, the last regular player to play pro baseball barehanded.

BUCK AND SPARKY

Let's go back to 1897, a very good year for the Reds, who finished twenty games above .500 under Buck Ewing, one of the most underrated mangers in Reds history. Ewing managed the Reds for five seasons, and they finished over .500 every time. The only other Cincinnati manager to claim a run of five straight winning seasons is Sparky Anderson. But none of Ewing's clubs ever won a championship, and the great Ewing—who is in the Hall of Fame for his play as a catcher—has long been forgotten by most Reds fans. One of the most thrilling games of that 1897 season came on Opening Day when the Reds staged a dramatic tenth-inning rally to beat the Cubs. And many in the crowd of eleven thousand, which was a sell-

THE TALENTED AND UNDERRATED CATCHER-MANAGER W.B. "BUCK" EWING

out, must have appreciated the new courtesy the Reds extended their fans that season. With the bicycle craze sweeping the nation, the club announced that fans could leave their bicycles inside the ballpark, where a club employee would keep a careful watch on the two-wheelers.

TWINS AND PRETZELS

The Reds made a serious run for the pennant in 1898. On August 7, they led by five games. But over the last two months, Boston and Baltimore caught up and Cincinnati dropped to third. The Reds pennant push was led in part by Pink Hawley's twenty-seven wins. Hawley, whose real name was Emerson, was one of identical twins; his parents, forever confusing the two babies, pinned a blue ribbon to one child and a pink one to the other. I'm not sure what happened to Blue, but Pink had a fine major league career, including his twenty-seven-win season for the Reds. The Reds had another interesting nickname working that season—the combination of pitcher Ted Breitenstein and catcher Heinie Peitz. Whenever Breitenstein pitched and Peitz caught they were known as the "Pretzel Battery," a nickname they picked up eating pretzels at a saloon. The Pretzel Battery was never better than on April 22, 1898, when Breitenstein threw a no-hitter. Peitz, of course, was his catcher. And you can see the scorebook of this historic game when you visit the Reds Hall of Fame.

UNSUNG JAKE BECKLEY

The Reds in 1899 had a record of 83-67, which in today's schedule, works out to be ninety wins, but they finished sixth in the twelve-team National League. Of course, the Reds season was far better than the miserable record of Cleveland, which set the all-time mark for futility in baseball by winning just twenty games and losing 134. The club was so bad that no one would come out to watch them at home, and so Cleveland played nearly all their games on the road. They wound up the season in Cincinnati, where, on the final day of the year, and in the final games of the nineteenth century, the Reds beat them in a doubleheader, 16-1 and 19-3. Playing first base for the Reds that season was Jake Beckley, who is one of the most over-looked stars in Reds history. He played six and a half years in Cincinnati and hit .325, which ranks him third on the all-time Reds list. Beckley was elected to Cooperstown in 1971 but curiously has never been enshrined in the Reds Hall.

JAKE BECKLEY PLAYED 2,368 GAMES AT FIRST BASE, A MAJOR LEAGUE RECORD
THAT STOOD UNTIL 1994, WHEN IT WAS BROKEN BY EDDIE MURRAY.

DOUBLEHEADERS

Veteran Reds fans will fondly recall the days when doubleheaders were a regular part of the major league schedule; nothing like two games for the price of one, and a full day of baseball at old Crosley Field. Doubleheaders are rare these days. Here's another rarity when it comes to doubleheaders: two games in one day—against two different clubs. On June 11, 1899, the Reds played Louisville in the first game, and immediately following that game they played Cleveland. Only one admission was charged, and there were eighty-two hundred fans on hand. The Reds must have enjoyed the unusual scheduling because they won both games, the second won by Reds Hall of Famer Noodles Hahn.

CINCINNATI

THE PALACE OF
THE FANS

FROM THE PALACE
TO THE WORLD SERIES

1900-1919

THE GRANDSTAND FIRE

It was the start of the new century, but the Reds had a lackluster season in 1900, finishing in seventh place, some thirty-six and a half games out of first. A fire in the grandstand early in the season provided the most excitement. The grandstand, built in 1894, was supposed to be fireproof, but in the middle of the night on May 28, the seats caught fire. The likely cause: a smoldering cigar that had fallen into the cracks in the floor. As the fire alarms sounded, nearby neighbors rushed to the scene, and many climbed into the outfield seats for a good view of the action! Despite the efforts of the fire department, the big grandstand burned to the ground, and the Reds suddenly found themselves without a home field. The club announced it would extend its upcoming road trip until a temporary diamond in the right-field corner of the ballpark could be built. One month after the fire, the new diamond opened, but groundskeeper John Schwab didn't have enough time to grow grass.

The infield was completely bare. And that wasn't the only unusual sight; the rubble of the old stands had not yet been cleared away. And for some reason they didn't fence it off. Believe it or not, any ball hit into the ruins was a live ball. The outfielders just had to dig it out.

THE BURNED GRANDSTANDS, AS RENDERED BY AN ILLUSTRATOR FOR THE *CINCINNATI ENQUIRER*.

A UNIFORM PROBLEM

No one was injured in the grandstand fire in 1900, although the team's mascot, a St. Bernard dog, did succumb in the blaze. But the flames destroyed all of the Reds uniforms. In their first few games after the fire, on the road they wore the home team's visiting uniforms while waiting for their new ones. But the wait turned into a battle over who would pay for the new gear. At that time, the players paid for their own uniforms, and the club wanted them to foot the bill. But the Reds players said, "No!" It was hardly their fault the park burned down. It finally took some help from the New York Giants to resolve the impasse. When Reds ownership asked the Giants for permission to use their traveling uniforms, the New Yorkers, in a show of player solidarity, refused to hand them over. With no uniforms, and faced with the prospect of having to forfeit several games, the Reds owner finally backed down and agreed to foot the bill for new duds.

HAHN AND CRAWFORD

In 1901, the Reds had their third-worst season in club history, winning just fifty-two games, and finishing last. They played on a makeshift field the entire 1901 season, due to the fire that destroyed the main grandstand behind home plate the year before. A new grandstand, which eventually would be known as the Palace of the Fans, was supposed to be finished during the 1901 season, but delays postponed the opening to the next year. Although the club finished in last place, the Reds featured two league-leading performers that year. Pitcher Noodles Hahn led in strikeouts, and outfielder Sam Crawford hit a league-best sixteen home runs. Crawford played four seasons in Cincinnati and would have stayed for more, but the Reds lost him to the new American League when the major leagues expanded in 1903. Crawford's accomplishments here are not forgotten; he was elected to the Reds Hall of Fame in 1968, and his plaque also hangs in Cooperstown, one of seventeen Reds Hall of Famers who are also honored at the National Baseball Hall of Fame.

A PALACE FOR THE FANS

The Reds finished an even .500 in 1902, which you wouldn't think would be so rare, but they have only managed to do that three times in club history. They were at seventy wins and seventy losses in 1902's 140-game schedule. But the big news was the opening of the new grandstand, which featured a very distinctive design and was nicknamed "Palace of the Fans." The Palace held about three thousand seats, including nineteen box-seat areas, called "Fashion Boxes." They extended out in front of the main grandstand and resembled boxes found in a classical concert hall more than traditional baseball seats. And while the Fashion Boxes held the upper crust of Cincinnati, immediately beneath them was the rowdy bleacher element. The grandstand sat some ten feet off the ground, and in the space below, at ground level, the club sold cheap standing-room tickets and plenty of beer. No doubt those enjoying the fine box seats above probably heard more than their share of ballpark…"entertainment," shall we say?

THE ORNATE FACADE OF THE SHORT-LIVED PALACE OF THE FANS WAS ONE OF THE MOST DISTINCTIVE OF ANY BALLPARK EVER BUILT.

THE CRANKS CHEER THE RHINELANDERS?

In the early 1900s, the Reds were often referred to as the Rhinelanders, a nod to the German heritage of the city. But other clubs also went by names that seem amusing today. When the Cubs came to play at the Palace of the Fans in 1902, they were known as the Orphans. The old Boston franchise, now the Braves, was fondly known as the Beaneaters. And if you had seen this in a headline, would you know which teams were playing: "The Highlanders Down the Naps?" That would have been the Yankees beating the Indians. The Perfectos and the Superbas? That was the Cardinals and the Dodgers. And did the fans enjoy the games? Well, the "fans" didn't because they weren't called "fans" then. That term wasn't used much until after 1910. The spectators of the early 1900s? They were called "cranks." And given the Reds record in the early 1900s, there were presumably a lot of very cranky fans.

REDS FOR SALE

In the long history of the Reds, only one owner has been from out of town: John Brush, a department store proprietor from Indianapolis. Brush bought the Reds in 1890 and, among other accomplishments, built the distinctive Palace of the Fans grandstand. By 1902 Brush was looking to sell, and he began negotiating with a syndicate of local owners, including the city water commissioner, Garry Herrmann, who would become the club's new president. The negotiations included the grandstands, the player contracts, and the franchise rights. The Herrmann group finally settled for $146,000, less than half of what the major-league minimum contract is for a player today. The actual check is still in existence—and on display at the Reds Hall of Fame.

REDS PRESIDENT GARRY HERRMANN WAS ONE OF THE MOST POWERFUL
MEN IN BASEBALL IN THE EARLY DECADES OF THE TWENTIETH CENTURY.

THE FIRST BATTLE OF OHIO

The year 1903 marks the first season of the World Series. The representative of the new American League, which was formed in 1901, was the Boston Pilgrims, now known as the Red Sox, who defeated the National League's Pittsburgh Pirates. The Reds were not to be found at the World Series that year, having finished fourth in the NL. But the Reds did participate in post-season play in 1903, facing off against Cleveland in a series of exhibition games after the season ended. This was billed as the "Battle of Ohio" and was a best-of-eleven affair. Games were held in Cincinnati and Cleveland, and also Columbus and Newark. Cleveland won the series, six games to three. The final games were played in a doubleheader in Cincinnati. The Reds won the first game and were leading 1-0 in the seventh inning of the nightcap when darkness fell. With Cincinnati ahead, the Reds faithful began clamoring for the umpire to call the game. Some of the most faithful walked out onto the diamond and set their scorecards on fire to demonstrate their displeasure. Unmoved by this impressive display, the umpire and police shooed the fireflys off the field, and Cleveland went on to score the winning runs.

ONE HOME RUN AWAY

If there was ever a time to not root for a Reds player to hit a home run, it was in 1905, when late in the season Reds outfielder Cy Seymour was on the verge of accomplishing one of baseball's rarest achievements: winning the triple crown. Seymour led the league in average and RBIs and was tied for the lead in home runs with teammate Fred Odwell. If Seymour remained tied for the lead or won the home run title outright, he would win the triple crown. But in the next-to-last game of the year, Odwell slashed a long drive to the outfield for an inside-the-park home run. Seymour wound up second, and he missed winning the triple crown by just the one homer. Only thirteen players have ever won the triple crown, and Cy Seymour came the closest of any Red.

PRINCESS ALICE

Once upon a time there was a Princess in the Palace…. Sounds like the start of a fairy tale, but it is a baseball story, really. The year was 1905, when the Cincinnati ballpark was called the Palace of the Fans. On June 8, the Reds entertained a very special visitor, Princess Alice, that is Alice Roosevelt, the daughter of the president of the United States, Teddy Roosevelt. Alice was twenty, attractive, rambunctious, full of opinions, and the press loved her. Her father said about her, "I can either manage the country or manage Alice. I can't do both." In today's magazine world, she would probably be on the cover of every grocery store tabloid and number one on the internet search engines. Her attendance at the game in Cincinnati was a major social event. She took her seat in box thirty-two along with her escort and future husband, Cincinnatian Nicholas Longworth. Some fans were quoted later saying they wish she hadn't come because they couldn't see around her large hat. The Reds won that day for the princess, 11-2, but their 1905 season had few other highpoints. They finished fifth, twenty-six games out of first place.

WOW! IT'S A HOME RUN!

Although there is a timeless quality to baseball, when you read a statistic like this next one, it makes you realize just how much the game has changed. In 1906, the eight teams in the National League combined for a total of 126 home runs, about sixteen home runs each! Not each player, each team. And that is the record for the fewest home runs hit in one year in the National League, coming at a time when the ball was relatively soft and didn't travel as far as today, and the ballparks were huge. For example, in the Palace of the Fans, it was farther down the right field line than it is to center field today in Great American Ball Park. No wonder nearly every home run then was inside-the-park. And the Reds in 1906? Well, no team had a chance that season against the Cubs, who won a record 116 games. In fact the great season of the Cubs, combined with a sixth-place showing by the Reds, left Cincinnati fifty-one games—yes, I said fifty-one games—out of first place, by far the most games the Reds ever finished behind the leader.

"SILLY" SHINGUARDS

In 1907, the Reds opened the season with a dramatic ninth-inning comeback to win the Opener over the Pirates, and . . . well, they should have stopped there. They wound up in sixth place, finishing twenty-one games under .500. Not much to cheer for at the old ballpark, but the faithful were treated to an interesting sight on June 18 when catcher George Schlei became the first Red to wear shinguards. Schlei was no doubt interested in experimenting with the new equipment, which New York Giant's catcher Roger Bresnahan had first used a few weeks earlier. But the Cincinnati crowd apparently didn't appreciate the innovation. The *Enquirer* reported that Schlei drew catcalls from the stands, and that it was the sentiment of everybody that he should remove the "silly shinguards" since they reduced the catcher's mobility. Despite the negative reviews, the shinguards became a long-running hit in baseball. Within a short time all clubs adopted them.

ROOT, ROOT, ROOT FOR THE HOME TEAM

In 1908, both pennant races went down to the final day of the season, thus earning that campaign the reputation as one of the greatest ever. But the Reds were nowhere to be found, finishing a distant fifth in the National League, twenty-six games out of first place. But Reds fans had something new to capture their fancy. In 1908, a couple of songwriters, hoping to capitalize on the growing popularity of baseball, wrote a new song, "Take Me Out to the Ball Game." The original featured the tale of a young female fan named Katie Casey who longed for nothing more than to go to the ballpark, yell at the umpire, and root on her team by singing the popular chorus. The song became baseball's unofficial anthem, and it was never more enthusiastically sung than by the Wrigley Field fans, led by the legendary broadcaster Harry Caray and his many guest singers, who included on one occasion, our own Marty and Joe.

FIRST LATIN PLAYERS

Back in the early days of baseball, player salaries were just a few thousand dollars, and teams were eager to play exhibition games to earn a few more bucks. In the fall of 1908, led by their business manager, Frank Bancroft, the Reds traveled all the way to Havana after the regular season ended to play exhibitions in Cuba. This was one of the first times a major league team had played in Cuba, and their visit helped spark baseball fever in Latin players. In fact, three years later, two Cuban players, Armando Marsans and Ralfael Almeida, appeared in a Reds uniform, becoming the first Latin players to play major league baseball in the twentieth century. Marsans became a regular outfielder for the Reds for two seasons and hit .317 in 1912. Almeida was a utility infielder for three years. Both players were inducted into the Cuban Baseball Hall of Fame.

DID YOU BRING THE TUBA?

Reds fans love their home opener, and 1909 was one season when the Opening Day festivities were the highlight of the season. The Reds finished in fourth place with no star players or other noteworthy achievements. But Opening Day, well, that was reason enough to be a Reds fan even as far back as 1909. Now, this was in the day before the folks at Findlay Market had started organizing the parade and pre-game festivities, and so the fans created their own celebrations on Opening Day. They formed rooter's groups, which met downtown on the morning of the opener. Many of the rooters carried musical instruments and noisemakers as they paraded through the streets in cars and horse-drawn wagons—not in any organized fashion, mind you, just up and down the streets, singing and rattling their noisemakers and no doubt stopping for refreshments along the way. It sounds like one big roving tailgate party. Eventually, the rooters wound their way out to the ballpark, marched around the field a couple of times and made their way to the seats. And after all that, they watched the game. Now, that's an Opening Day!

STOLEN BASES

In 1910, when the Reds played in their big ballpark called Palace of the Fans, the home run was certainly not a part of their offense. The fence distances were very deep, and nearly every home run hit in this park was of the inside-the-fence variety. The big fields and the dead ball created a lot of emphasis on the running game, and the one statistic that jumps out at you from that season was in the stolen base column. The Reds stole 310 bases that year, which is the all-time club record for one season. To put that in perspective, in recent times, the club has peaked around 190 stolen bases. Even in the heyday of the Big Red Machine, with Joe Morgan, Ken Griffey, Sr. and Dave

BOB BESCHER'S 81 STEALS IN 1911 REMAIN THE TEAM RECORD.

Concepcion, the club never had more than 210 steals, a hundred less than that 1910 club. Who were the theft leaders back then? Players you probably have never heard of: Bob Bescher, Dode Paskert, and Hans Lobert. But all their running didn't seem to have much impact. The Reds couldn't steal the pennant. The 1910 Reds finished fifth, twenty-nine games out of first.

GENTLEMAN, START YOUR RUNNERS

In Indianapolis they held the first Indy 500 in 1911, and in Cincinnati, a few days after the great race, the baseball fans must have wondered if they were watching their own race of some sort. Runners were rounding the bases in record-breaking fashion. On June 3 and 4, the Reds played the Boston Braves, and over these two games, Reds runners circled the bases for a total of forty-one runs, which is still the modern club record. On June 3, the Reds won 15-4, but the offense was just getting warmed up. The next day, they buried the Braves, 26-3. The first seven runs were scored before anyone was out, and the Reds led, 15-0, after four innings. They scored the final nine runs after two were out in the eighth. The Boston newspaper headlined the game: "Full Account of the Murder: Cincinnati Kills Boston 26-3 Before 7,000 Witnesses." It was the high point of the year for the Reds, who wound up in sixth place.

LAST GAME AT THE PALACE

Remember all the buildup to the last game at Cinergy Field? The game drew a standing-room-only crowd on September 22, 2002. And then there was the reunion softball game that brought back the stars of Riverfront, including Pete Rose, for an encore. Quite a contrast then, to look back at the final game of Cincinnati's historic Palace of the Fans ballpark, which closed in 1911. A whopping crowd of just 424 showed up for the final game. In fact, they started demolishing parts of the grandstand a month before the season ended. Ironic that the park closed with a whimper, for today the Palace is recognized as one of the most distinctive grandstands ever built. But at the time, they couldn't wait to tear it down. Nothing much left of that old park, but there is one of the seats from the Palace on display at the Reds Hall of Fame.

A VIEW OF THE DEMOLISHED PALACE OF THE FANS

OF SHIPS AND BALLPARKS

On April 10, 1912, the *Titanic*, a brand new ship, left England for New York on her maiden voyage. Coincidentally, the Cincinnati Reds launched a new enterprise the day after. On April 11, just four days before the *Titanic* would sink after hitting an iceberg, the Reds opened a new ballpark, which one reporter liked so much he called it a "magnificent baseball resort." The new park, called Redland Field and later named Crosley Field, got off to a rousing start with a victory on Opening Day and a visit a few weeks later by a famous Cincinnati native, President William Howard Taft. Taft became the first sitting president to see a game in Cincinnati. Then on May 18, the club held formal dedication ceremonies and invited dignitaries from the baseball world to a grand dedication dinner. The dinner was a lavish affair with the VIPs seated around a massive square table decorated as a baseball diamond. But all the attention did little to improve the fortune of the Reds in 1912. They finished fourth, twenty-nine games out of first place. But at least they were losing in a magnificent new resort!

HERRMANN FIELD?

When the Reds new ballpark opened in 1912, it didn't have an official name. Many fans encouraged the owner of the Reds at the time, Garry Herrmann, to name it after himself. If he had, we might remember that park as Hermann Field. After all, several new ballparks at the time had been named after their owners: Wrigley Field in Chicago, Ebbets Field in Brooklyn. But Garry refused and eventually settled on the name of Redland Field, a tribute to the team's colors. It's unfortunate Herrmann didn't put his name on the park, as we would probably remember him more today. He was a very prominent owner in baseball history and served as what essentially was the first commissioner of baseball in the early 1900s. When Powel Crosley bought the club in 1934, the savvy businessman recognized an opportunity to promote his many consumer products, and he put his name on the ballpark. And today, we still remember it as Crosley Field.

GET OUT THE MOPS!

It is rare with today's state-of-the art fields that games are rained out. But in the old ballparks, wet weather caused many more problems. Let's go back to Opening Day in Cincinnati in 1913. A week-long storm system caused flooding throughout the Ohio Valley, and a week before the scheduled opener, the field was under twelve feet of water. After most of it drained away, the grounds crew swept out the remaining puddles and ran a steamroller over the field to wring it out. But the roller broke down, which was not surprising considering it had been sitting under water for several days. Finally, Matty Schwab, the legendary head groundskeeper, resorted to setting fires on the grass to dry out the field. By game time, the water was gone, but so was the grass. The field featured a few remaining spots of green turf, surrounded by black topsoil and sawdust. So much for a Field of Dreams! This was a nightmare. The flood also ruined the Reds clubhouse, and the team moved into the visitor's clubhouse, which left the visiting teams with no locker room. So the visiting players dressed in their hotel rooms uptown and travelled back and forth to the ballpark in full uniforms, which must not have been too pleasant after the games. The new clubhouse was finally finished in June.

JUST ONE BALL

Here's an obscure piece of trivia from the 1913 season and another reminder of how the game has changed over the years. In a game on June 29, the Reds beat the Cubs, 9-6. Nothing unusual there, but the *Cincinnati Enquirer* reported that the teams played with only **one** ball. In these early years of baseball, it was typical for just a few balls to be used during a game. They didn't replace balls as often as today. Scuff marks, dirt—they kept using the ball. And foul balls into the stands were usually returned to the field. But to make it through an entire game with one ball? That was enough to catch the attention of the reporter. "The ball was pretty badly battered," he wrote, but to his eyes, it was still good enough to use in extra innings if the Cubs had tied the score. Reds manager Joe Tinker took the ball home as a souvenir.

WHO'S THE ROOKIE?

Not much was expected of the Reds in 1914, and they certainly lived up—or down—to expectations, finishing thirty-four games under .500, in last place. And they capped off the 1914 season with a disastrous nineteen-game losing streak, the longest in club history. But that losing streak was not the worst thing to happen that year. For in 1914, the Reds turned down Babe Ruth. How did that happen? Well, that season, the Reds had the opportunity to sign two players off a Baltimore minor league club. The Reds sent a scout to Baltimore who brought back a shortstop and an outfielder while somehow overlooking a nineteen-year-old pitcher by the name of Ruth. The Babe wasn't a slugger yet. He began his career as a pitcher, so perhaps the Reds just weren't interested in a young rookie twirler. But the guys they did pick, well, you never heard of them: George Twombly and Claud Derrick, who between them, wound up with exactly one home run—just 713 behind the Babe.

RUBE THE DAREDEVIL

SPEED DEMON RUBE BENTON

Rube Benton pitched nine seasons for the Reds in the early 1900s and had a fifteen-year career in the major leagues. It is amazing he lasted that long. Benton had a passion for speed and not just on his fastball. In 1914, riding a motorcycle, Benton was hit by a car, and a few weeks later, traveling at high speed, he crashed into a streetcar in Cincinnati. The second wreck left him with a broken jaw and a concussion, and the club ordered him to sell his motorcycle. Teammate Heinie Groh offered to buy it, but changed his mind when he took it for a test drive around the ballpark and crashed into the tarpaulin when the brakes failed. Twelve years after his retirement from baseball, Benton died…in an automobile crash at the age of fifty.

GET YOUR HALL OF FAMERS HERE!

CHRISTY MATHEWSON DOFTS HIS CAP TO ADORING FANS.

The Reds pulled off one of the most unusual trades in baseball history in 1916 in a five-player deal with the Giants. It essentially involved a trade of managers. The Reds traded their player-manager, Buck Herzog, and in exchange picked up the aging superstar Christy Mathewson, whose pitching days were almost over. But the Reds didn't want him as a pitcher; they named him the new manager of the club. In the deal, the Reds also received Bill McKechnie and Edd Roush, two familiar names to Cincinnati fans. At the time McKechnie was a so-so infielder, but after his playing days were over, he had far more success as a manager, including nine seasons in Cincinnati. Roush, of course, became the starting center fielder and helped lead the Reds to the 1919 World Series. Coincidentally, all three players the Reds received in the deal, Mathewson,

EDD ROUSH WAS ONE OF THE NATIONAL LEAGUE'S MOST FEARED HITTERS
FROM THE LATE TEENS THROUGH THE ROARING '20S.

McKechnie, and Roush, are in the Hall of Fame in Cooperstown, making this the only time in baseball history three Hall of Famers were traded in one deal. Unfortunately, the influx of new talent didn't do much for the Reds in 1916, as the club finished in seventh place. The star player for Cincinnati that year was Hal Chase, better known for his gambling and charges of fixing games. But in 1916, Chase became the first Red to lead the league in hitting, with a .339 average.

GROH'S BOTTLE

Any mention of the Hall of Fame can easily start arguments over which players aren't in Cooperstown but should be. And the Reds have several candidates on the bubble. Bucky Walters, Dave Concepcion, and Vada Pinson are among the Reds who have received significant support but not quite enough. Add to the list Heinie Groh, the Reds third baseman from 1913 to 1921. Groh is best remembered today for his bat, an odd-shaped, big-barreled stick of lumber nicknamed the "bottle bat." But Groh was also an All-Star-caliber third baseman. He is, with little argument, the greatest third baseman in Reds history. He was the offensive leader of the Reds 1919 World Championship club. He later went to the New York Giants and was the starting third baseman on their championship teams. In 1922 he hit .474 in the World Series. In retirement, Groh lived in Cincinnati, and he celebrated that World Series by using 474 as his license plate number.

HEINIE GROH, AN UNDERRATED STAR FOR THE REDS, WIELDS HIS FAMOUS BOTTLE BAT.

DOUBLE NO-NOS

The Reds never challenged for the pennant in 1917 and finished in fourth place, not a particularly notable season, except for a very unusual no-hit game on May 2 of that year. In Chicago, Cubs pitcher Hippo Vaughn threw a no-hitter against the

FRED TONEY WON TWENTY-FOUR GAMES AND POSTED A 2.20 ERA IN 1917.

Reds for nine innings. What made it memorable, however, was that Reds pitcher Fred Toney was matching Vaughn batter for batter. Both pitchers had a no-hitter going after nine innings. Finally, in the top of the tenth, Reds shortstop Larry Kopf singled for the first hit of the game. Kopf scored moments later on an error and an infield hit to give the Reds a 1-0 lead. In the bottom of the tenth, Toney kept his no-hitter intact by retiring the side in order, and baseball had its first and only double no-hitter. What is it about the Reds and no-hitters? Especially no-hitters in pairs. First there was this "double no-no" in 1917, and then there was Johnny Vander Meer's two no-hitters in consecutive starts in 1938. Then there was the back-to-back no hitters at Crosley Field in 1969. Jim Maloney of the Reds threw one against the Astros on April 30, and the next night Don Wilson of the Astros no-hit Cincinnati. When it comes to no-hitters, the Reds like seeing double!

WHO'S ON FIRST?

The Reds finished third in 1918, despite having Hal Chase, one of baseball's most questionable figures, as their first baseman. Chase was often suspected of trying to fix games, and on July 25 he did conspire with one of his teammates, Lee Magee, to

NOW KNOWN MOSTLY FOR THROWING GAMES, HAL CHASE WAS AN OUTSTANDING HITTER AND WAS CONSIDERED THE TOP FIELDING FIRST BASEMAN OF HIS ERA.

try to lose a game against Boston. But the whole affair was a comedy of errors that eventually led to both of them being banned from baseball. If the Three Stooges had tried to fix a game, it couldn't have turned out any worse. The game was tied in the thirteenth when, with two outs, Magee bounced softly to short. Should have been the third out, but the ball took a bad hop, and Magee, who didn't want to be on base, was safe at first. He then tried to steal second. Not surprisingly, he got a terrible jump and should have been an easy out, but the catcher made a wild throw and now Magee found himself in scoring position. Edd Roush, the next hitter, then hit a long drive, and Magee watched hopelessly as the ball landed beyond the outfielders. He had to score, for Roush had clubbed an inside-the-park home run. The Reds held on in the bottom of the thirteenth to win the game. Magee had scored the winning run in a game he was trying to lose. Magee and Chase then made another big mistake; they paid the gamblers with a check, and after the game, Magee tried to stop payment. The gamblers blew the whistle on the ballplayers, and major league baseball eventually banned them both for life.

WAR VICTIM

One of the greatest pitchers of all time, Christy Mathewson, was also a manager of the Reds from 1916 to 1918. He might have managed the Reds World Series winners in 1919 if it hadn't been for a tragic incident in WWI. Mathewson joined the Army and was injured in a training accident in France, the victim of a gas attack. Mathewson was in the hospital as the 1919 season approached. The Reds tried to contact him by telegram but couldn't find him. The team finally hired Pat Moran, who led the Reds to a World Series win. Mathewson eventually returned home but never managed again. He suffered from tuberculosis as a result of the accident and died at the age of 47.

THE REDS FIRST NL PENNANT

The Reds won the World Series in 1919, but the season started with few hopes of a pennant. For one thing, the Reds had not been pennant contenders in over twenty years. And that spring, it didn't look like things would change. They held spring training in Waxahachie, Texas, just south of Dallas, and the weather was so wet the club struggled to find dry ground. At one point they worked out in a local graveyard. They had no regular first baseman, second baseman, or shortstop, and their pitching staff was thin. But new manager Pat Moran recommended several deals to the club, and nearly every one proved successful. The club jumped out to a fast start and suddenly the Reds were in the unusual position of pennant contenders. They finished 22-5 in July, and ran off a ten-game winning streak in August. These Reds were for real. They wound up with a 96-44 record, a winning percentage of .686. In the modern schedule of 162 games, that computes to 111 wins. Which is the best winning percentage in club history since 1900, better even than any of the Big Red Machine teams.

1919 WORLD SERIES

During the final weeks of the 1919 season, the Reds, who were leading the league and on their way to the NL pennant, began making plans for the World Series. There was enormous interest in ticket sales, but Redland Field held only twenty thousand seats, and the club wondered if a potential financial bonanza was slipping away. At that time, north of Cincinnati, in the suburb of Sharonville, there was a large speedway with seats for thousands of spectators, and the Reds considered using the infield of the big track as the ball field. They estimated they could add temporary seats for up to a hundred thousand people, which would have made this the best-attended World Series of all time. But the plans were scrapped, the Reds added some temporary seats to their ballpark, and the Series was held at Redland Field, but the 1919 World Series almost wound up at a racetrack.

HALL OF FAMER GREASY NEALE

Ever heard of Reds outfielder and Hall of Famer Greasy Neale? No? Well, it may be because Neale is enshrined in Canton, not Cooperstown. He's in the Pro Football Hall of Fame and not the baseball version. Now, Neale was a fine ballplayer. He was an outfielder for the Reds for eight seasons and was the starting right fielder for the 1919 World Champions. But his greatest success came on the gridiron as a coach and a player. He is the only man to play in a World Series, coach a team in the Rose Bowl, and coach a team to an NFL title.

MANAGERS KID GLEASON AND PAT MORAN SHAKE HANDS FOR THE CAMERAS BEFORE THE FIRST GAME OF THE 1919 WORLD SERIES.

LOCATION, LOCATION, LOCATION

When Jose Rijo made his comeback after several surgeries had robbed him of his dominating fastball and hard slider, he said he had become a "real estate" pitcher: location, location, location. Another pitcher who believed in this real-estate philosophy was Slim Sallee, one of the stars of the Reds 1919 championship season. Sallee, who lived in Higginsport, Ohio, about thirty-five miles east of Cincinnati, was suffering back problems late in his career when he joined the Reds at age thirty-four. Perhaps due to his injury, he excelled at getting the most out of the fewest pitches. In 228 innings in 1919, he walked only twenty batters, an average of less than one walk per nine innings. And in late September, he set a then-major league record by pitching a complete game using just sixty-five pitches! The game lasted all of fifty-five minutes.

THE REDS HOIST THE 1919 NATIONAL LEAGUE CHAMPIONSHIP BANNER.

WHERE ARE THE TROPHIES?

One of the most popular galleries at the Reds Hall of Fame is devoted to the many championship seasons of the Reds. Here is where you will find the World Series trophies from 1975, 1976, and 1990. Many visitors want to know: Where are the trophies from 1919 and 1940, the other years the Reds won the World Series? Well, the Hall of Fame doesn't have them on display because there never were any trophies from those seasons. Hard to believe, but the custom of baseball presenting an official trophy to the winning club did not begin until 1967. Called the "Commissioner's Trophy," it features flagpoles with the names of each club and the name of the winning team inscribed on the base. In the earlier years, the emphasis seems to have been on the large banners or pennants the clubs flew at their ballparks to boast of their championships.

WAKE UP, EDD!

A plaque of Edd Roush hangs in the Reds Hall of Fame gallery, and Roush is also a member of the National Baseball Hall of Fame in Cooperstown. In fact, Roush, a native of Oakland City, Indiana, near Evansville, was the first Red ever to be elected to Cooperstown. Roush led the league twice in hitting as a Red—the only other Cincinnati player to do that is Pete Rose. (Pete actually did it three times.) Roush was also a great outfielder, but he was once thrown out of a game for taking a nap in centerfield! At the Polo Grounds in New York, Reds manager Pat Moran got into a long, heated argument with the umpires. Standing in center field, and bored with the proceedings, Roush first sat down on the grass, then made a little pillow out of his cap and glove, and soon fell asleep. By the time the umpire called, "play ball," Edd was snoozing! His teammates yelled at him to wake up, but old Edd was in dreamland. His teammate and third baseman Heinie Groh walked out and jostled him awake. But the umpires, whose patience had been severely tested after the long argument, sent Edd to the showers for delaying the game.

POWEL CROSLEY, JR.

EDD, EPPA, AND POWEL

1920-1939

AN UNSUCCESSFUL DEFENSE

In 1920, for the first time in the club's history, the Reds were the defending World Champs. They returned most of the same players from their championship team, and they were in first place for over two months. But the Dodgers ran away with the pennant with a furious September finish, and the Reds slumped to third. That was a pivotal year in American history. It marked the beginning of prohibition, and women were given the right to vote. There were changes in baseball, as well, and one certainly worked against the Reds. The rule makers voted to ban any foreign substances used to alter the baseball. Some pitchers had used spit, sandpaper, paraffin, files, and other objects to scuff up the ball; the marring of the surface helped them throw pitches that curved and broke sharply. Two of the Reds' most successful pitchers in 1919, Hod Eller and Slim Sallee, often relied on these "trick" pitches. But with the new rules, both suffered a decline, and so did the Reds, unable to defend their title.

TRIPLEHEADER

Did you know the Reds hold the modern National League record for most games played in one day? The Reds played a tripleheader back in 1920 at the end of the season in Pittsburgh. The tripleheader was necessary because games had been rained out earlier in the season. Normally, the clubs wouldn't have had to make them up, but the extra games were necessary because the Pirates and the Reds were fighting for third place and the extra money that went with winning that spot. To allow

THE 1920 BAN ON DOCTORING THE BASEBALL DOOMED THE CAREER OF HOD ELLER,
A STAR OF THE 1919 REDS.

enough time for the games, in this era before night baseball, the clubs started the tripleheader at noon. The Reds won the first two games and clinched third place; the Pirates won the final game, which was called after six innings due to darkness. Reds pitcher Hod Eller had a very good day, but not on the mound. He started one game at first base and the next game at second base and went four for seven.

LONG BALL

Edd Roush and Heinie Groh were two of the stars of the Reds in the early 1920s, and when they both decided to hold out in 1921, well, the season was over before

it started. Roush didn't report until May 1, and Groh held out a month longer. Without their stars, the Reds struggled offensively and wound up in sixth place. Nineteen twenty-one is perhaps better remembered as the year the long ball came to Cincinnati. The Reds had been playing in Redland Field for ten years, and in those ten seasons, no one…not one batter…had hit a ball over the fence on a fly. The long distances and the dead ball meant that all home runs had been inside the park. But on May 22, in a game between two Negro League teams who were renting the ballpark for their

EDD ROUSH SHOWS THE STANCE THAT MADE HIM ONE OF THE GREATEST HITTERS IN REDS HISTORY.

exhibition, John Beckwith became the first player to hit one over the left-field wall. Two weeks later, Reds outfielder Pat Duncan became the first to do it in an official major league contest. One fan was so surprised he ran to a nearby florist and brought back a bouquet of flowers for the home run hero and presented them to Duncan in the middle of the game.

THREE-BAGGERS

The Reds had a very strong team in 1922, led by two Hall of Famers, center fielder Edd Roush and pitcher Eppa Rixey. The Reds wound up second, seven games behind the New York Giants. The Reds played in Redland Field, later to be renamed Crosley Field in the 1930s, and Redland Field at that time was enormous. It was 350 feet or more down each foul line and over 420 feet to center field. Consequently, there were few over-the-fence home runs but a lot of triples. In the early years of baseball, it was common for teams to hit more triples than home runs. The Reds hit ninety-nine three-baggers that season and only forty-five homers. Even the older guys got in on the action. First baseman Jake Daubert, a member of the Reds Hall of Fame, had twenty-two triples that season, at the age of thirty-seven. That guy could motor. Of course, today the triple is on baseball's endangered list. Teams hit about six times as many home runs as triples in the smaller ballparks. Interesting, isn't it? As players have gotten bigger and stronger, the parks have grown smaller. We love the long ball, but baseball has paid for it at the expense of one of the most exciting plays: the triple.

THE PRIDE OF HAVANA

Nineteen twenty-three was the year of Dolf Luque, a Cuban-born pitcher whose nickname was the "Pride of Havana." And Luque made Havana proud that year. By some measures, his 1923 season ranks among the top seasons ever by any pitch-

DESPITE HIS SMALL STATURE, PITCHER DOLF LUQUE INTIMIDATED HITTERS
WITH HIS FIERY TEMPER.

er. At 5'7" and 160 pounds, Luque did not have a dominating physique, but he was tough as nails. A bulldog of a competitor, he certainly was in enough brawls to prove it. His dark skin color often provoked taunts from other clubs, and Luque was not afraid to retaliate with a punch or a brushback pitch that left the offender in the dust and might have also emptied the dugouts. That 1923 Reds club had several other outstanding pitchers including Hall of Famer Eppa Rixey, but Luque single-handedly kept the Reds in the pennant chase that summer. His season totals: twenty-seven wins, eight losses and a 1.93 ERA. He started and won both games of a doubleheader. At one point he racked up twenty-nine scoreless innings in a row. And somehow he even managed to pick up two saves! His Reds finished second, but Luque wound up number one for his pitching performance.

HOLDOUTS

You don't hear much about holdouts in baseball anymore, when players stay home from spring training in hopes of getting a salary increase. But in baseball's early years, this was a common tactic for players to use, and one of the Reds who often resorted to the holdout was center fielder Edd Roush. Roush didn't care much for spring training to start with, and he didn't seem to need it, with a batting average that hovered around .350. In 1922, Roush didn't sign until July 23, and he only played in fifty games. After another holdout in 1923, the Reds tried a new strategy with their stubborn star, and they signed Roush to a three-year contract, believed to be the first multi-year deal in club history. The salary for the star center fielder: nineteen thousand dollars a year.

THE REDS ARE ON THE RADIO

On Opening Day in 1923 the Reds reached an important milestone: it was the team's first broadcast on radio. There was no broadcast booth, so the announcer just sat at a small table on the roof of the grandstand. And WLW didn't bother to hire a sports announcer because there really weren't any yet. Eugene Mittendorf, one of the station's music announcers, handled the play-by-play. For the record, WLW and WSAI both carried that first game—and with no commercials that we know of. This custom remained in place for the next few years. WLW broadcast just one game each season, the opener, although one of the announcers in 1926, 1927, and 1928 was none other than Powel Crosley, the founder of WLW and the future owner of the Reds. WLW began expanded coverage in 1929, but the club wouldn't allow Sunday home games to be carried live. They were afraid it would hurt attendance. It wasn't until 1949 that every game was broadcast.

A TRAGIC SEASON

The 1924 season got off to a dreadful start. During spring training, manager Pat Moran fell ill from a kidney disease and a week later he died. The forty-eight-year-old

**REDS MANAGER
JACK HENDRICKS**

Moran had led the Reds to their World Series win in 1919 and was very popular in Cincinnati. He was replaced by Jack Hendricks, who had just been added to the club as a coach. Some players earn the phrase "clubhouse lawyer" for their constant squabbling, but, in Hendricks case, he truly deserved the title. Hendricks actually had a law degree from Northwestern. The club rallied behind Hendricks and started the season with a win on Opening Day before a record crowd of 35,747, which was the biggest Opening Day crowd ever at old Crosley Field. The Reds remained in contention most of the season but finished fourth, ten games out of first place. After the season was over, friends of Pat Moran had a large bronze plaque made to honor the late manager and it hung at Crosley Field for many years. Today it hangs in the Reds Hall of Fame.

TRAGIC SEASON, PART TWO

Pat Moran's death at the start of the 1924 season was enough tragedy in one year for any team, but 1924 proved doubly tragic. First baseman Jake Daubert, one of the first team captains in Reds history, died at the end of the season. The forty-year-old Daubert, who played on the Reds 1919 championship team, was nearing the end of his career. He debuted with the Dodgers in 1910 and quickly established himself as an excellent defensive player and hitter. He wound up his fifteen-year career with a .303 average. He was still the starting first baseman of the Reds in 1924 when he suffered a serious beaning that left him dizzy for several weeks. Then he developed a rare spleen disorder and in his weakened condition, declined rapidly. Wanting to be with his teammates as the season ended, he traveled from his native West Virginia to Cincinnati for the final game of the 1924 season but was so weak he could not return home. He died a few days later, a death met with tremendous sadness throughout baseball.

THE SURPRISING DEATH OF POPULAR FIRST BASEMAN JAKE DAUBERT, A LEADER ON THE 1919 CHAMPIONSHIP TEAM, SADDENED REDS FANS AND PLAYERS.

PUTTING THE "WET" IN "BAN-QUET"

The year was 1925, and what a pitching staff the Reds had: Eppa Rixey, Pete Donohue, Dolf Luque. The Reds finished first in the league in ERA and led the league in shutouts. But as it turned out, they would have had to throw a shutout every game for this team to win. Their offense finished dead last in scoring, and even with all the great pitching, the Reds could do no better than third place, fifteen games behind the champion Pirates. Reds owner Garry Herrmann provided some off-field headlines when he had twenty-five barrels of beer delivered to a hotel in St. Louis during a road trip. Prohibition was still going strong in 1925, and the local authorities confiscated the brew. Herrmann and his pals wound up paying a hefty fine. It was said about the affable Herrmann that he put the "wet" in "banquet."

LOMBARDI AND HARGRAVE

Can you name a Reds catcher who won a batting title? If you said Ernie Lombardi, you are correct, but he isn't the only one. In 1926, Bubbles Hargrave won the title while catching for the Reds. He hit .353. Hargrave and Lombardi are not just the only Reds catchers to win a batting crown, they are the only two catchers ever to led the National League in hitting. In 131 seasons, the only two catchers ever. Lombardi is in the Hall of Fame in Cooperstown, and both are in the Reds Hall of Fame.

HUGH CRITZ

If you ask Reds fans to pick the club's all-time best second baseman, no doubt the choice would be Joe Morgan, the Hall of Famer who played for Cincinnati from 1972 to 1980. But before Morgan, who is your pick? In 1969, on the hundredth anniversary of professional baseball in Cincinnati, fans voted for their all-time Reds

**THE REDS 1925 PITCHING STAFF WAS AMONG THE VERY BEST IN TEAM HISTORY.
(L-R): NEAL BRADY, HARRY BIEMILER, TOM SHEEHAN, EPPA RIXEY,
PETE DONOHUE, RUBE BENTON, CARL MAYS, DOLF LUQUE, AND JAKIE MAY**

SLICK-FIELDING HUGH CRITZ

team, and the winner at second base was Hugh Critz, a slick-fielding infielder from the 1920s, who beat out such favorites as Johnny Temple and Lonnie Frey. Critz wasn't much of a hitter, but he was widely regarded as the best fielding second baseman, and his reputation was known throughout the league. In 1930, the *Sporting News* called him "perhaps the greatest fielding second baseman" of all time. Critz was elected to the Reds Hall of Fame in 1962, and you'll see his plaque the next time you visit.

WINGO AND THE SPHINX

Here is a record not likely to be broken. Reds catcher Ivy Wingo, who played for the Reds from 1915 to 1926, retired with the distinction of having caught the most games in baseball history. But that isn't the record we're talking about. His games-caught mark has long-since been broken. No, Wingo's moment of destiny occurred in Egypt, when the catcher was on a world tour to promote baseball. On a dare, he wound up and threw a ball completely over the giant statue of the Sphinx. Wingo's toss over the Sphinx's head has apparently never been matched. Something to try on your next trip to Cairo.

MORE SEATS FOR REDLAND

One of the milestone years in baseball was 1927, the year the Babe hit sixty home runs and the famous 1927 Yankees swept the World Series. In 1927, the Dow

Jones hit a high of one hundred. Yes, the 1920s were roaring, although the 1927 Reds were more of a whimper than a roar. After several years of being in contention, the 1927 club faded to fifth. There was one major change at the ballpark. With the success of the team in previous years, owner Garry Herrmann installed additional seats, field-level boxes that stretched all around the base of the original grandstand. They added about five thousand extra seats to the capacity of the park. The expansion forced the club to move home plate out from the new seats, some twenty feet. Herrmann also decided to add some additional revenue. He added an extra row of advertising signs to the wall in left field, making the wall a huge double-decked billboard. It was Herrmann's last hurrah. Due to ill-health, he retired at the end of the season. Herrmann owned the Reds for twenty-five years, the second-longest tenure of any Reds owner.

FEW HOMERS AT REDLAND

Looking back at some of the statistics from the early days of Crosley Field, it is surprising to see how few home runs were hit there. Those of us who watched baseball at Crosley in the '40s, '50s and '60s recall it as a good hitter's park, with plenty of long ball action. But it wasn't always so. When the park first opened in 1912, the distance from home plate to the fences was much longer; in fact, veteran *Cincinnati Enquirer* sports writer Jack Ryder couldn't imagine there would ever be a ball hit over the fence at the new park. Ryder wasn't crazy; in fact, it was ten years before the Reds Pat Duncan hit the first over-the-fence home run in a major league game. What happened that finally turned Crosley into the "cozy confines?" In 1927, the club added field-level box seats and moved home plate out some twenty feet. Then, in 1938, the club moved home plate out another twenty feet to further shorten the distances. This helped make left field (328 feet) and center field (383 feet) more homer friendly, but what about right field? Even with all the changes, it was still a whopping 366 feet down the line.

HISTORIC EVENTS

Baseball has been a part of the lives of Cincinnati fans since the 1860s. And when baseball season starts, well, that's all a lot of Reds fans ever pay attention to from April to September. But, of course, despite what we all sometimes think, the world doesn't stand still for Reds baseball. Significant historical events have their way of intruding on the daily box scores. For example, Opening Day 1912 at Cincinnati's new ballpark, Redland Field, occurred just three days before the sinking of the *Titanic*. Or, in 1944, D-Day was on June 6 in the middle of the season, and all games were cancelled as President Roosevelt urged Americans to spend the day in prayer. Back in May of 1927, Charles Lindbergh became the first person to fly across the Atlantic Ocean, an event that captivated the nation. Lindbergh returned to a hero's welcome and in August he was welcomed to Cincinnati with a ten-mile-long parade and a ceremony at Redland Field. How big a deal was it? The Reds postponed their game with the Phillies and played a doubleheader the next day.

KNOCKING DOWN THE FENCES IN BOSTON

You may have heard the phrase "knocking down the fences" applied to home run hitters, but the Reds actually accomplished this feat once in a round-about way. In 1928, Rogers Hornsby was traded to the Boston Braves, and Boston installed temporary seats in left field to bring the fence in closer hoping to benefit from Hornsby's home run power. The great Hornsby, however, was not having a good year, and visiting teams seemed to be getting all the advantage from the shortened fence. The Reds visited Boston in June, and in the first game pitcher Ray Kolp homered into the new seats. The next day it was pitcher Pete Donohue, and in the third game it was the big right hander Eppa Rixey. That was enough for Boston management. When three pitchers hit home runs over the short porch, it was time to knock the fence down. And that's exactly what they did.

FREAK INJURIES DOOM THE REDS

The Reds of the 1920s featured a strong pitching staff, and with Eppa Rixey and Red Lucas leading the way in 1928, the team got off to a fast start. Heading into late May the Reds were in first place, but then two odd injuries dashed their hopes. The first happened on May 27 when Lucas suffered a broken wrist. He was hit by a ball—*during batting practice*. And if that wasn't bad enough, four days later their leading hitter, center fielder Ethan Allen, (no relation to the furniture maker, by the way), suffered a broken cheek bone when we was beaned. And this happened during an exhibition game! During this era, it was not unusual for clubs to play exhibitions on their off-days, and the Reds had stopped in Buffalo, New York, on

EPPA RIXEY HOLDS THE TEAM RECORDS FOR VICTORIES, GAMES STARTED, AND INNINGS PITCHED.

their way east. Allen was hit in the noggin and wound up missing several games. The Reds quickly faded from contention and finished fifth. The one highlight in that 1928 season was the double-play combination of second baseman Hugh Critz and shortstop Hod Ford. The two helped lead the Reds to the then NL record of 194 double plays in one season and that is still the club record.

THE GREAT REDS DEPRESSION

Nineteen twenty-nine is probably best remembered for the crash of the stock market and the beginning of the Great Depression, which would last throughout the

1930s. Coincidentally, the fortunes of the Reds seem to follow the same path. After a very successful run in the 1920s, when the Reds contended for the pennant several times, 1929 marked the end of their success. The 1929 Reds finished 66-88 and started a string of sub-.500 seasons that would create a depression of its own for Reds fans. It wasn't until 1938 that the Reds again had a winning season. One highlight from that 1929 season was the play of right fielder Curt Walker, who is largely forgotten by fans today. But Walker's career statistics with the Reds closely mirror those of another, more familiar right fielder, Ken Griffey, Sr.. Walker was the starting right fielder for six seasons, Griffey

FORGOTTEN SLUGGER CURT WALKER

for seven. They had similar slugging percentages and on-base percentages; Walker had 482 RBIs with the Reds, Griffey, 466, and they had identical batting averages with the Reds of 303., which ties them for tenth place on the all-time Reds list.

TAKE ME OUT TO THE BRAWL-PARK

In 1929, the Reds entered the summer months struggling to stay out of last place. Attendance was down and interest in the club was fading, until they engaged in a big brawl with the Cubs in Chicago. Hack Wilson, one of the Cubs best players, fought with two Reds pitchers, and the news was splashed all over the front pages. Players issued threats and warnings, and suddenly the next Chicago-Cincinnati series began to take on great importance. There was bound to be a brawl! We'll get even with those Cubbies! The next time the clubs met was in Cincinnati, and fans bought up tickets by the handful. Of course, the teams were as polite as butlers. Nary a harsh word or a punch thrown. The fans might have been disappointed, but management was thrilled. In the middle of a losing season, the Reds drew 35,432 to the brawl-park, the largest regular-season crowd in Reds history to that point.

OH, WHAT MIGHT HAVE BEEN!

This familiar lament of many players and fans over the years can even apply to owners. Sidney Weil of Cincinnati purchased the Reds in 1929 and could very well have become the most successful owner in Reds history had it not been for an off-the-field event Weil had no control over, the collapse of the Stock Market. Weil lost much of his fortune, and when the opportunity arose, he couldn't afford to sign a promising young player by the name of Joe DiMaggio. Weil might also have gone down in history as the innovator of night baseball. He installed lights at the Reds minor league club in Peoria in the early 1930s, but he ran out of money and was forced to sell the

Reds before he could erect lights in Cincinnati, leaving that honor for the next ownership team, general manger Larry MacPhail and owner Powel Crosley.

DAPPER DAN

The Reds of 1930 managed to combine average pitching with a pitiful offense to finish in seventh place in the eight-team league. They won just 38 percent of their games, one of their worst records in history. The manager of this unfortunate clan was Dan Howley, whose nickname was "Dapper Dan" because he was such a sharp dresser. But no matter how good Howley looked, it didn't translate into winning baseball. Howley managed the Reds for three seasons, three remarkably consistent and awful seasons. He was 59-95 in 1930, 58-96 in 1931, and 60-94 in 1932. One of those seasons was enough to get most managers fired, but three of them? This was so bad, it was truly historic. He has the worst record in Reds history by a huge margin. But Howley and his Reds did witness one historic moment that season when right fielder Curt Walker became the first Red to ever hit an over-the-fence home run into the right-field bleachers at old Redland Field. The park had opened in 1912, so it took eighteen years for a Red to accomplish this feat. Why did it take so long? Because the distance to the bleachers was over four hundred feet, the typical distance to deep center field these days.

OLD-TIMERS TO THE RESCUE

In 1931, the Empire State building had just opened in New York. Cincinnati's own skyscraper, Carew Tower, also opened that year, and the Reds in 1931, well, they wished they had never opened at all. They lost seventeen of their first nineteen games. The Reds were in the cellar by the end of April and remained in last place for the rest of the season. They drew all of 263,000 fans to the ballpark, an average of about 3,400 a game. Perhaps realizing the fans were never coming out to watch this team play, the Reds decided to hold an Old-Timers Game at the ballpark on September 5, and over fifty former players attended, including pitchers Slim Sallee and Hod Eller from the 1919 champion Reds, and the great Cy Young, the winningest pitcher in all baseball history, who pitched one inning. But it was seventy-one-year-old Arlie Latham, who had last played for the Reds in 1895, who stole the show with an around-the-bases dash that ended, ala Pete Rose, with a slide into third base that left the old-timer dazed but the crowd on its feet. Finally...something to cheer about in 1931.

PITCHER AND SHORTSTOP?

Most of the players in the Reds Hall of Fame are honored for their excellence in hitting or pitching, but there is one player who is in the Hall for both: Red Lucas, a pitcher from the 1920s and 1930s who was also a fine hitter. Lucas won 109 games for the Reds, which ranks him fifteenth in club history. He also managed to hit .281 in his career and was often used as a pinch-hitter. He still holds the Reds club record with eighty pinch hits. Lucas also appeared as an outfielder and an infielder for the Reds, playing third base, second base, and even shortstop! Think about that. Can you imagine seeing a pitcher today used as a shortstop?

BY THE NUMBERS

In June of 1932, the Reds started a tradition that has become so commonplace we don't even think about it anymore. On June 26, 1932, the Reds appeared on the field with numbers on their uniforms. They weren't the first club to do it; the Yankees earned that distinction in 1929. The other American League clubs followed in 1931, and the NL mandated numbers in 1932. Among the more historic numbers handed out that day were ones eventually to be retired, including number five, made famous by Johnny Bench, which was first worn by Babe Hermann.

Number ten, Sparky Anderson's number, was first worn by Leo Durocher. The number eight of Joe Morgan was worn by Wally Roettger. But most interesting was the number eighteen, first seen on the back of pitcher Eppa Rixey. That number later became Ted Kluszewski's number, and the Reds retired it in 1998. Rixey, who is in the Hall of Fame in Cooperstown, never had a number in his heyday in the 1920s, and the club does not recognize him with a retired number. However, at the end of his career he did wear number eighteen, and so perhaps Big Klu wouldn't mind sharing the spotlight and let the fans also recall one of the greatest Reds pitchers of all time, Eppa Rixey, when they see the big eighteen behind home plate at Great American Ball Park.

THANK YOU, SID WEIL

In 1933, Cincinnati's Union Terminal was dedicated two weeks before the opening of the baseball season, and today this Art Deco classic houses the Cincinnati Museum Center. And frankly, it is better to recall this famous Cincinnati landmark than to recall the dreadful 1933 season endured by the fans of the Reds, who suffered through a last-place finish. The Reds wound up thirty-three games out of first place. The Reds owner at the time was Sidney Weil, who at the end of the season was forced to sell the club because of financial difficulties. But Weil was around long enough to make two deals that eventually helped the Reds to the pennants in 1939 and 1940. In 1932, Weil brought in a young catcher named Ernie Lombardi, and in 1933, he made a deal with the Cardinals for a bulldog of a young pitcher named Paul Derringer. Certainly to Reds fans of 1933, Derringer didn't exactly look like much of a pitcher. He won just seven games and lost twenty-five. Those twenty-five losses are the most suffered by any Reds pitcher since 1900, but his record was deceiving. Derringer's ERA was actually under the league average! His teammates just couldn't score any runs. But by the late 1930s, when the offense finally blossomed, so did Derringer, becoming one of the all-time greats in Reds history.

SID WEIL WAS AN INVENTIVE AND ENERGETIC OWNER, BUT THE STOCK MARKET CRASH
DOOMED HIS CHANCES OF BRINGING A WINNER TO CINCINNATI.

NUXHALL AND QUINN

Name the youngest player in modern baseball history. Most Reds fans immediately know that one—Joe Nuxhall, the native of Hamilton, Ohio, who debuted with the Reds at the tender age of fifteen in 1944. But do you know who was the oldest pitcher to play for the Reds? He was Jack Quinn, who pitched for the Reds in 1933 at the age of fifty. Quinn made his debut in 1909. He played almost his whole career in the American League with New York, Boston, and Philadelphia. Altogether he pitched twenty-three seasons. He must have had a very durable arm, for even at age forty-four he pitched over two hundred innings! He finished his career with 247 wins, to rank in the top fifty all-time in baseball history. When the Reds signed him in 1933, he was only forty-nine; surely he had something left! He had a decent record in relief, pitching 15 $^2/_3$ innings with a respectable ERA of 4.02. He pitched his final game on July 7, two days after his fiftieth birthday.

SI JOHNSON, NEARLY PERFECT

Twenty-seven up and twenty-seven down. Those are the stats of a perfect game, and Tom Browning is the only Red's pitcher to accomplish that milestone. But there was another Reds hurler who faced only twenty-seven batters in one game, but you've probably never heard of him. Si Johnson pitched for the Reds from 1928 to 1936 and nearly joined Browning as a Reds legend for all time on May 4, 1933. Johnson retired the side in order in the first inning and gave up a single in the second. The runner was then caught stealing, and from that point on, Johnson did not give up another hit. He did not walk anyone, nor were there any errors. In all,

SI JOHNSON, NEARLY IMMORTAL

he faced just twenty-seven hitters, the absolute minimum. But that one hit kept him from a perfect game. And to add even more frustration, Johnson threw another one-hitter two weeks later. If Johnson had gotten either one of those two out, or both of them, he would be as well known in Reds lore as Browning or Johnny Vander Meer.

RED BARBER

In 1934, a young broadcaster moved to Cincinnati from Florida to begin his base-ball play-by-play career. Red Barber was hired by new Reds owner Powel Crosley even though Barber had never seen a major league game. There were no major league clubs within hundreds of miles of Barber's home, and the young redhead

RED BARBER DELIGHTED REDS FANS IN THE 1930S WITH HIS
COLORFUL DESCRIPTIONS OF THE GAMES.

had learned his craft broadcasting college sports. After he was hired by WLW, Barber watched some spring training action and prepared for his first broadcast on Opening Day, 1934. Just before the opener began, Barber noticed WLW newscaster Peter Grant take a seat in the rear of the booth. Seems as though Powel Crosley wanted someone there to back up Barber in case Red couldn't do the job. But Barber's talent was soon evident, and Grant left after a couple of innings, confident that the new kid in the booth could handle things just fine, thank you! Barber left the Reds in 1938 and went on to broadcast for the Dodgers and the Yankees, becoming one of baseball's legends. He is one of two Reds play-by-play announcers honored by the National Baseball Hall of Fame in Cooperstown. The other? Marty Brennaman.

GOING, GOING, GONE!

"There's a long drive, and the ball is going, going, gone!" That is a familiar call for many baseball announcers, and it appears that the "going, going, gone," phrase originated right here in Cincinnati in the 1930s. It was popularized by an announcer named Harry Hartman, one of the first play-by-play announcers in Reds history. Hartman, who also called boxing and wrestling matches and other sporting events, began calling Reds action in 1929. He was a familiar voice all throughout the 1930s, broadcasting on WCPO in competition with Red Barber, who was on WSAI. In the 1930s, the Reds were on more than one station because the club did not grant exclusive broadcast rights to one station until 1945. Hartman more than held his own against Barber, twice winning a national poll conducted by The *Sporting News* as the best baseball broadcaster. "Going, going, gone" was his trademark call, along with "Bam" and "Socko" for hard hit balls, and a "can of corn" for an easy pop fly.

NIGHT BASEBALL

Hard to imagine today that night baseball, now so popular, could have ever been questioned. Yet when the Reds first proposed it back in 1935, the other major league owners opposed the idea. They thought it was undignified, that there was a carnival atmosphere associated with night-time entertainment that was beneath the dignity of the grand old game. The owners also feared that the lights wouldn't be bright enough, that the fans and the players wouldn't be able to follow the ball. But Reds owner Powel Crosley and general manager Larry MacPhail kept arguing that night baseball was worth a try. The owners finally agreed, but barely. They only allowed the Reds to play seven night games that first year, one against every other National League team. The first night game in major league history was played on May 24. The Reds beat the Phillies that night, 2-1, as 632 lights blazed on at Crosley Field. The light towers became a permanent fixture at the ballpark, changing its appearance forever. The Reds investment paid off in its first year. The club drew an average of 18,620 to its night games, while day games were averaging just over 4,600.

THE TERRACE

Other than playing the first night games in major league history, the Reds didn't do much on the field in 1935, finishing sixth. But it was a significant season for another change at Crosley Field, one just as memorable as the light towers for Reds fans—the extension of the left-field terrace into center field and right field. The left-field terrace had been there ever since the ballpark opened in 1912. It was a natural part of the landscape of the field, and it provided a bank of seating for overflow crowds. But the terrace ended in left-center field. Then came the wild night game of July 31, 1935, when a huge crowd filled the park and many stood on the field. The terrace was packed with fans, but thousands more stood along the foul lines and up against the fences. Afterward the club decided to extend the terrace all the way around the outfield to provide more temporary seating. To this day, Crosley Field is remembered for its unique terrace.

HALL OF FAMERS IN THE LINEUP

You would think having four Hall of Famers on your roster would make you a pretty good team. Case in point: the 1970s, when the Reds featured three everyday players in the lineup who eventually made it to Cooperstown—Bench, Morgan, and Perez, and one more, Pete Rose, who would surely be there if it weren't for his suspension from baseball. The only other time the Reds featured four Hall of Famers on their roster was in 1935. The future Hall of Famers included catcher Ernie Lombardi, first baseman Jim Bottomley, and outfielders Kiki Cuyler and Chick Hafey. But with the exception of Lombardi, all were nearing the end of their careers and their value was negligible. The Reds finished a dismal sixth, thirty-one and a half games behind the Cubs.

THE BABE AND THE BABES

The big news in spring training in 1936 was an attempt by the Reds general manger Larry MacPhail to lure Babe Ruth out of retirement. Ruth was offered a

BABE RUTH

chance to pinch-hit for the Reds, but he turned down the deal, saying he had put on too much weight in the off-season and didn't think he could get in shape. Without the Bambino to attract the fans, MacPhail turned to other strategies, including the hiring of attractive young "usherettes" to roam the stands and sell candy and cigarettes. The young women wore silky, dark blue pants with white berets; MacPhail referred to them as lounging "pajamas," perhaps not the best way to describe the uniforms to his conservative Midwest audience. The usherettes lasted only one season. MacPhail also outfitted his team in colored pants, adding bright red satiny trousers to the Reds ensemble for night games, thinking the pants would be very colorful and reflective under the lights. But they proved to be so hot the players didn't like them, and the hot pants soon disappeared from the wardrobes.

STARS AT CROSLEY

In 1938, the Reds hosted the All-Star Game in Cincinnati. The first All-Star Game was in 1933, so this was the sixth annual affair, and Cincinnati turned out a capacity crowd of over 27,000 at Crosley Field. Many had come to see not the established

A CAPACITY CROWD GATHERED FOR THE 1938 ALL-STAR GAME AT CROSLEY FIELD.

stars, but the Reds young pitching sensation Johnny Vander Meer, who was starting for the National League. Just a month earlier, Vandy had tossed his back-to-back no hitters and earned the start. He lived up to his billing, pitching three shutout innings and earning the victory, as the National League triumphed, 4-1. The highlight of the game came on an oddball play: with the score 2-0 in the seventh, NL shortstop Leo

THE REDS VERSION OF MURDERERS ROW IN 1938: ERNIE LOMBARDI, WALLY BERGER, IVAL GOODMAN, AND FRANK McCORMICK

Durocher put down a sacrifice bunt and it turned into a home run! There were two errors on overthrows, and Durocher wound up circling the bases. The Reds had three players voted into the starting lineup: outfielder Ival Goodman, catcher Ernie Lombardi, and first baseman Frank McCormick. All in all, the Cincinnati fans watched twenty-six players, coaches, and managers who would one day become Cooperstown Hall of Famers. And that didn't count the home plate umpire, the famous Bill Klem.

THE BABE RUTH OF THE REDS

Baseball experienced quite a power surge in the 1930s. Babe Ruth had popularized the home run in the 1920s, and by the 1930s balls were flying out of parks at a record pace. Except, that is, in Cincinnati at Crosley Field. In the early 1930s, you were lucky to ever see a home run at Crosley. The Reds hit only five home runs at home in 1933! Finally in 1938, the club decided to join the home run bandwagon and moved home plate out twenty feet to shorten the distance to the fences. And the first home run star of the Reds was born: Ival Goodman, the Reds outfielder. He set a new club record in 1938 with thirty home runs, which must have seemed like sixty would to us today.

PENNANT CLINCHER

The St. Louis Cardinals were favored to win the pennant in 1939, and the Reds were seen as contenders, although nobody was picking them to win. After all, it had been twenty years since they had last won a pennant. But the club got off to a fast start, took over first place in late May, and battled the Cardinals down the stretch. The fever of the pennant race caused the Reds to make a major addition to Crosley Field that summer. In August, the club began extending the upper deck of the grandstands all the way out the foul lines to have the addition ready for the World Series. But the Reds still had to hold off the Cardinals, and in late September, nursing a two-and-a-half-game lead, they met St. Louis at Crosley Field for a show-down series. The Reds needed just one win to clinch, and they sent twenty-four-game winner Paul Derringer to the mound on September 28. Veteran Crosley Field fans claim it was one of the most thrilling games they ever saw. Derringer was hardly sharp; he was racked for fourteen hits. He was supported by a couple of outstanding defensive plays, and the Reds hung on to clinch the pennant with a 5-3 win.

TELEVISION DEBUT

The Reds have a fascinating radio history, going all the way back to the 1920s, but did you know that the Reds pioneered televised baseball? It happened on August 26, 1939 at Ebbets Field in Brooklyn, and Dodger announcer Red Barber called the play-by-play. It seems unlikely that anyone who saw that first broadcast thought baseball on TV could ever succeed. The screens were very small, and one newspaper writer noted that while you could see the players move around, you couldn't see the ball. For the record, the first batter on television was Cincinnati third baseman Billy Werber, and the winning pitcher in the first televised game was the Reds Bucky Walters. And the advertiser? Well, that was a Cincinnati story too. It was Procter and Gamble's Ivory Soap.

REDS ACES PAUL DERRINGER AND BUCKY WALTERS

MANAGER BILL McKECHNIE, THE GUIDING FORCE BEHIND
THE BACK-TO-BACK PENNANTS

THE "DEACON"

There are two Reds managers honored in the Hall of Fame in Cooperstown: Sparky Anderson and Bill McKechnie, who guided the 1939-1940 Reds to two National League pennants and a World Series win. McKechnie's nickname was "Deacon," which should give you some idea about his personality and managing style. He wasn't the fiery type, more of an easy-to-get-along-with manager. He liked to say, "You'll catch more flies with honey than you will with vinegar." But he had a tough side as well. It was said of the Deacon that he could teach Sunday School on Sunday and go toe-to-toe with an umpire on Monday.

TRIPLE CROWN

Only one Cincinnati Reds pitcher is in Cooperstown, and that is Eppa Rixey. But the pitcher with the next best case would be Bucky Walters. Walters wound up with 198 career victories. He helped lead the Reds to a World Championship in 1940, he led the league in wins three times, he won two ERA titles, and in 1939, he was voted the National League MVP. That year, Bucky won the pitching triple crown, leading the league in wins, ERA, and strikeouts. Ironically, it was not his pitching that kept him out of Cooperstown. It was the years he spent at third base. Walters started his career as an infielder, and, well, he wasn't very good. By the time he converted to pitching, he was twenty-six years old. He made a fast transition, but his career pitching totals suffered. If he could have won another thirty or forty games, he might be in Cooperstown today. But his plaque does hang in the Reds Hall of Fame.

SCHNOZZ

He was the "Schnozz," a fond nickname for one of the all-time great Reds, catcher Ernie Lombardi, he of the very prominent nose. But despite the nose, Lom (he was a man of many nicknames), was exceptionally popular with the ladies, who would crowd into Crosley Field on Ladies Days—remember those?—to watch the big catcher. Lombardi held most of the hitting records for a Reds catcher until Johnny Bench came along. He was probably the most popular Red ever in the era of old Crosley Field. And so when the Reds finally made it to the World Series in 1939, with Lom behind the plate, Cincinnati fans just knew their favorite Red would shine. But Lombardi and his teammates couldn't handle the Yankees pitching, and the Reds lost in four straight to one of the great Yankee teams of all time. Not only did the Yankees sweep, but Lombardi suffered a humiliating injury when he was knocked out cold in a collision at home plate in Game Four. Stunned, Lombardi lay on the ground near home plate with the ball just a few feet away, while Joe DiMaggio ran all the way home from third base. Certainly Lombardi

was not at fault, yet the headlines in the paper called it "Lombardi's Snooze." For years the image persisted, and many baseball experts felt it long delayed his election to the National Baseball Hall of Fame. Lom was finally elected in 1985, nine years after his death. But he fared better in Cincinnati. The Reds made him one of the original five players elected to the Reds Hall of Fame, and you'll see his plaque there when you visit the Hall of Fame gallery at Great American Ball Park.

LADIES MAN ERNIE LOMBARDI

THE FINAL OUT OF THE 1940
WORLD SERIES

FROM BUCKY
TO BIG KLU

1940-1959

THE JUNGLE CLUB

When third baseman Bill Werber joined the Reds in 1939, he was impressed with the hustle and ability of his new teammates in the infield, especially second baseman Lonnie Frey and shortstop Billy Myers. The three began calling themselves the "Jungle Club" for their agility and fierce determination on defense. They gave themselves nicknames: Jaguar, Tiger, Leopard. First baseman Frank McCormick soon wanted to be included in the club, but Werber thought McCormick needed to

BILL WERBER LED THE REDS WITH A .370 AVERAGE IN THE 1940 WORLD SERIES.

show more hustle. Soon Frank was diving for ground balls and running out every hit. "Okay, Frank, you're in the club," the guys told him. "Great," said McCormick. "I want my nickname to be Wildcat." "Well, Frank," the guys told him, "you're kind of slow, so your nickname is Hippo." The gullible McCormick was fit to be tied. All that hard work and he's going to be known as "Hippo." After considerable teasing, his teammates relented and "Hippo" became "Wildcat," part of a spirited infield defense that helped lead the Reds to the 1940 World Championship.

UMPS FOR A DAY

Imagine big league players running to first base on a grounder, and the umpire waiting there to call the play is a member on his own team! Well, that is exactly what happened on May 13, 1940, at Crosley Field in a game between the Reds and the Cardinals. Because of a scheduling mix-up, the National League failed to assign umpires to the game. With a big ladies-day crowd of nearly sixteen thousand fans pouring into the ballpark, the Reds management scrambled to find a solution. Fortunately, Larry Goetz, a major league umpire living in Cincinnati, happened to be at home, and he was pressed into emergency service. But they still needed base umpires, and the managers agreed to allow Reds coach Jimmy Wilson and Cardinals pitcher Lon Warneke to become umpires for a day. With Wilson and Warneke handling the bases, the game finally started thirty minutes late. The two fill-in umps each received a fifty-dollar bonus from the National League for their emergency duty. And, there were no rhubarbs.

NO CAKEWALK

In that championship season of 1940, the Reds appeared to have been a very dominant team. They ran away with the pennant by twelve games in September, and won one hundred games for the first time in club history. But that 1940 team overcame a great deal of adversity. The most tragic was the suicide of back-up catcher Willard Hershberger in early August. No one was sure how the club would respond to this most awful of baseball tragedies. The Reds also had to play without Johnny Vander Meer for most of that season, although Vander Meer's issues were more conventional. He simply didn't pitch well. He was sent back to the minors and only pitched in ten games. The Reds had their aces, Paul Derringer and Bucky Walters, at the top of the rotation, but they didn't have a lot of depth with Vandy back in the minors. Fortunately, another youngster, Gene Thompson, handled the pennant pressure admirably and became a solid third starter. One thing that didn't need fixing was the defense. That 1940 Reds team set the then National League fielding record with a .981 percentage.

THE REDS REGULARS BEFORE GAME ONE OF THE 1940 WORLD SERIES:
(L-R): BILL WERBER, MIKE McCORMICK, IVAL GOODMAN, FRANK McCORMICK,
JIMMY RIPPLE, ERNIE LOMBARDI, EDDIE JOOST, BILLY MYERS, LONNIE FREY

GAME SEVEN HEROES

In club history, the Reds have only played in three World Series Game Sevens. They lost one, in 1972, and won the others, each by one run, in 1940 and 1975. Many Reds fans today recall that Joe Morgan drove in the winning run in 1975 with a bloop single to center field in the ninth inning that beat the Red Sox. But who was the hero of Game Seven in 1940? Well, it was Billy Myers, the Reds shortstop. Cincinnati trailed Detroit, 1-0, in the seventh inning when the Reds rallied to tie the score and had the go-ahead run on third with one out. The Tigers elected to walk Ernie Lombardi and face Myers, who had struggled offensively in the Series. But Myers lofted a long fly to centerfield that easily scored Jimmy Ripple with what proved to be the winning run. Joe Morgan and Billy Myers, linked forever in Reds lore with their Game Seven championship hits.

**THE WINNING RUN SCORED SECONDS AFTER THIS PHOTO WAS TAKEN.
JIMMY RIPPLE HEADS BACK TO THIRD TO TAG UP AND HEAD FOR HOME ON THE FLY
TO CENTER BY BILLY MYERS.**

BIRDIE AND HUTCH

In the 1940 World Series, the Detroit Tigers had two players who eventually wound up managing the Reds: Fred Hutchinson and Birdie Tebbetts. From 1954 to 1958, Tebbetts guided the Reds and holds the distinction of being the only philosophy major to ever manage the club, although there are many who claim all good managers must have been philosophy majors. Tebbetts managed the powerful Reds team of 1956, and to this day, one of the rookies on that team still credits Birdie with helping him get off to a great start in his career: Frank Robinson. By the way, the nickname Birdie? It came from his high squeaky voice. Hutchinson, of course, managed the Reds to the 1961 World Series and was one of the club's most popular skippers. Tragically, he fell ill with cancer during the 1964 season and died in November of that year.

NUMBER FIVE TRIBUTE

In the summer of 1940, the Reds were in the middle of a hot pennant race with Brooklyn, when catcher Ernie Lombardi suffered an injury, and backup catcher Willard Hershberger was forced into the lineup. The Reds lost a couple of close games, and Hershberger, who was at times moody and prone to depression, blamed himself for the defeats. He committed suicide in a hotel room in Boston on August 3, the only major league player to ever do so during a season. The club announced they would retire his number five in his honor. But by the end of the season, they had issued number five to another player and the promise was forgotten. In 1967, number five was assigned to a young rookie named Johnny Bench, and after Bench's great seventeen-year career, the Reds retired number five for good. And so it remains today, on the grandstand façade behind home plate at Great American Ball Park, a tribute to Bench's great career, and a silent reminder of the tragic end of Willard Hershberger.

1940 CELEBRATION

The 1940 World Series ended with Game Seven in Cincinnati, and a victory over the Detroit Tigers that sent the town into a frenzy. Downtown business workers filled the streets. The fans returning from Crosley Field joined the melee at Fountain Square on adjacent corners. Ticker-tape rained down from the office buildings. Auto horns blared and streetcar bells clanged throughout downtown. But fans became a little too boisterous; they tipped over a streetcar and police had to close many streets. It was the first time in any city that a World Series victory was followed by a major civic disruption, something that has become all too familiar in recent years following championship sporting events.

JIMMY WILSON (HOLDING BOTTLE) AND MIKE McCORMICK HOIST PAUL DERRINGER ON THEIR SHOULDERS WHILE WARREN GILES GRABS HIS HAND DURING THE LOCKER ROOM CELEBRATION AFTER THE WORLD SERIES VICTORY.

ERNIE LOMBARDI WELCOMES HOME FRANK McCORMICK DURING THE 1941 SEASON OPENER.

DIMAGGIO GRABS THE HEADLINES

The Reds were the defending world champs, and with their pitching staff led by Bucky Walters, Paul Derringer, and Johnny Vander Meer, they were picked by most to repeat. But the offense struggled all season, and the Reds never mounted a serious charge at first place, although they wound up with a fine 88-66 record in third place. Over in the American League, the big news was the fifty-six-game hitting streak of young Joe DiMaggio. As the streak reached thirty games and beyond, it became front-page news. The first question of the day was not "Did the Reds win?" but "Did Joe get another hit?" The streak began on May 15; it reached forty games on June 28; it reached fifty games on July 11. And it finally ended on July 17 in Cleveland in front of 67,000 fans at old Memorial Stadium, the largest crowd to see a game in the big leagues that year. And on the West Side of Cincinnati in the summer of 1941, the Rose family was tending to their newborn son, not ever imagining that young Pete would, thirty-seven years later, become the next player to seriously challenge DiMaggio's streak

CHANGES BUFFET THE REDS

As the 1942 season opened, the Reds were only two years removed from their 1940 World Championship and still had the core of a strong pitching staff. But the loss of several key players, including catcher Ernie Lombardi, who was sold to the Boston Braves, took its toll. And more importantly America's entry into World War II, after the bombing of Pearl Harbor on December 7, 1941, suddenly changed the baseball landscape. Many young players enlisted, and many more were drafted. Reds historian Lee Allen wrote that the scouts "stopped asking whether a player could run or throw and asked instead about his draft classification and whether he had three dependents or a punctured eardrum." All the ball clubs worked to support the war effort, and the Reds posted patriotic signs on the outfield walls: "Remember Pearl Harbor," "Keep Fit," "Avoid Waste," and "For Victory, Buy Defense Bonds and Stamps." The Reds young players—filling in for Billy Myers,

Bill Werber, and others who had left the team—were simply not ready. The pitching staff was second best in the league, but the offense collapsed. The Reds wound up with a team batting average of just .231, one of their lowest in history.

NOTHING TO IT!

In September of the modern baseball season, the active roster expands to forty players, and a lot of young minor leaguers are called up for their first appearance in the big leagues. And how cool would it to be to hit a home run in your first at-bat? Well, it almost happened to Reds rookie Chris Denorfia in 2005 when he homered in his second at-bat. But first at-bat home runs have only happened twice in Reds history. In 1950, Ted Tappe hit a pinch-hit home run against the Brooklyn Dodgers. And in 1942, twenty-year old Clyde Vollmer did the ultimate, not only homering in his first at-bat, but hitting it on the first pitch he ever saw in the major leagues. And to make it even more special, Vollmer, a graduate of Western Hills High School in Cincinnati, did it in front of his hometown fans at Crosley Field. I hope they saw it, because it took Clyde quite a while to hit his second one. He missed the next few years in the service, and it wasn't until 1947, five years later, before Vollmer connected on his second home run. Vollmer went on to play ten seasons in the majors and wound up with sixty-nine homers, but none could have been as memorable as that first one.

WARTIME BASEBALL

World War II dominated the news and affected everything including, of course, the National Pastime. The Reds played exhibition games at army and naval training camps. All the clubs were ordered to conduct spring training north of the Ohio River to cut down on travel and help the nation's efforts to ration gasoline. The Reds moved their spring training site from Florida to the Indiana University campus in Bloomington. The club offered special discounts to soldiers and that helped set the all-time attendance record at Crosley Field of 38,017, thanks in part to two thousand servicemen and four hundred blood donors who were admitted free on August 29. On the field, the 1943 Reds were again led by a strong pitching staff, anchored by Johnny Vander Meer, Elmer Riddle, Bucky Walters, and Joe Beggs. The club wound up in second place, their best finish during the war years, but they had no shot at the pennant. They finished eighteen games behind the Cardinals who had one of the best seasons in National League history, winning 105 games.

Cincinnati Reds

FIRE-BALLER JOHNNY VANDER MEER, KNOWN THROUGHOUT HIS CAREER FOR DOMINATING SPEED AND ERRATIC CONTROL, TAKES AIM AT THE PLATE.

THE YOUNG LEFT-HANDER

Most Reds fans know Joe Nuxhall was the youngest player to appear in a major league game and that he made his debut in 1944. Actually, as it turned out, he wasn't the youngest ever. There were a couple of kids even younger than Joe who played briefly in the nineteenth century, but the old left hander still holds the honor for being the youngest since 1900. He debuted on June 10, 1944, at the age of fifteen… fifteen years, ten months, and eleven days to be exact. But that was not the first time he had been in uniform. That honor came on Opening Day 1944, when Joe sat on the bench and watched the Reds play the Cubs. Of course, he wasn't your ordinary ballplayer. The other players didn't have to get an excuse from their school principal to attend the game! But Joe did. I don't suppose principals hear that excuse too often: "Sir, the Cincinnati Reds want me to come and sit on the bench during the game today. They might use me to pitch." Actually, there wasn't much chance of Joe pitching that day. The Reds just wanted to invite him to the game and let him work out with the team. From his seat on the bench, Joe watched the Reds lose to the Cubs in that 1944 opener. The Reds finished a solid third that season but sixteen games behind the Cardinals, the very team Nuxhall debuted against on June 10.

FIFTEEN-YEAR-OLD JOE NUXHALL CHATS WITH MANAGER BILL McKECHNIE ON JUNE 10, 1944.

CLYDE WHO?

The roster of Reds no-hit pitchers includes Johnny Vander Meer, Tom Seaver, Tom Browning, and Clyde Shoun. Who? Clyde Shoun, a part-time starter with the Reds

in the early 1940s. At Crosley Field on May 15, 1944, Shoun no-hit the Boston Braves, nearly tossing a perfect game, allowing no hits and only one walk. Shoun was the most unlikely of pitchers to toss a no-hitter. Let alone a no-hitter, he hadn't thrown a shutout in four years! Interestingly, Shoun's masterpeice came just one day after the Reds Bucky Walters had thrown a one-hitter. Walters never did throw a no-hitter in his great career, nor did many other Reds stars including Eppa Rixey, Paul Derringer, and Jose Rijo. But on one day in 1944, Clyde Shoun was the best of all.

CLYDE SHOUN—KING FOR A DAY

ON A SHOESTRING

A lowly shoestring helped the Reds to an Opening Day victory over the Pirates in 1945, one of the most dramatic Opening Day games of all time. With two on in the fifth inning, one of the Pittsburgh base runners noticed his shoe was untied. He tried to call time out, but Reds pitcher Bucky Walters threw a pitch to the batter and—BAM!—he hit it for a three-run homer. The runners began circling the bases. But wait ...one of the umpires had signaled time out and the play didn't count. Given a second chance, the Reds got out of the inning with no runs being scored. The Reds then scored six runs to take the lead on a grand slam by outfielder Dain Clay. But the Pirates fought back to tie the game in the seventh. The contest went into extra innings, and Clay came through again in the eleventh, knocking in the winning run. Shoestrings, grand slams, and extra innings will make any opener a memorable one.

STOMP THAT SUCKER FLAT

The Reds finished seventh in 1945, the year World War II came to an end. Baseball attendance was on the upswing as the war years drew to a close, but not in Cincinnati. The Reds finished dead last in attendance in all of baseball and hit a low point late in the season when a game at Crosley Field on September 13 drew just 281...yes, that's right, 281 fans. One spectator who wished she hadn't gone to any game at Crosley Field that year was in the stands on June 19. Sitting near the Reds dugout, the young woman suddenly felt something brush her leg, and looking down she realized she was sharing her seat with a rat. Serious screaming soon broke out, and a rookie infielder for the Reds, eighteen-year-old Ralph Kraus, bolted out of the dugout, jumped over the railing, and smashed the little critter with his spikes. Kraus was the hero of the moment in what turned out to be the only "appearance" of his major league career. Kraus, a Cincinnati native who had played on the Bentley Post American Legion national championship team in 1944, never played in a game. The Reds sent him to the minors, and he never made it back to the big leagues.

NO HARD FEELINGS

We've all heard stories recently about fans and players mixing it up in verbal battles and even the occasional fight. But here's another twist on the story. During a game in 1945 at Crosley Field, umpire George Magerkurth, upset over the heckling he was enduring from some Reds fans, walked over to the box seats, exchanged some words with the fans, and then leaned over the rail and punched one of the Reds faithful. The fan, who was a former boxing referee from Dayton, wound up with lacerations and a black eye. He filed an assault-and-battery charge against Magerkurth, but later dropped the charges when the ump made a public apology and paid one hundred dollars for his medical expenses.

DEAF PLAYERS

There have been three deaf players in the big leagues and all had a Cincinnati connection. The first was Dummy Hoy, who was a Reds outfielder in the late 1800s and is in the Reds Hall of Fame. The second was Luther Taylor, a pitcher. Taylor never played for the Reds, but later in his life he was a coach at the Illinois School for the Deaf, where one of his players was Dick Sipek, who played for the Reds in 1945. Sipek was used as a pinch-hitter and an outfielder and hit .244. It was the only year he played in the big leagues.

NO OFFENSE

By the spring of 1946, World War II had finally ended, and fans looked forward to the first peacetime season in five long years. At home, moms and dads were producing a lot of little future fans. That year marked the start of the baby boomer generation. Fortunately, these little tykes were too young to understand what was happening at Crosley Field, for in 1946 the Reds made the fans cry all season. They had pretty solid pitching, led by Ewell Blackwell, Johnny Vander Meer, and Joe Beggs, but their offense was dead last. They just couldn't score runs. They set a club record with forty-one one-run defeats. They played a nineteen-inning scoreless tie, the longest nothing-to-nothing game in major league history. Even Hall of Fame manager Bill McKechnie couldn't figure this team out, and he resigned on September 22, marking the end of his nine-year run as manager, second-longest in club history. The Reds finished sixth, thirty games out of first place.

MR. BAD LUCK

Sometimes you can't catch a break in baseball, and that was true of the fifteen-year career of Ken Raffensberger, who pitched eight of those seasons with the Reds from 1947 to 1954. During those years, Raffensberger was usually among the club leaders in ERA and wins, but he didn't have much support. The Reds never had a winning season in those eight years, and that kind of bad luck dogged the big left-hander. Raffensberger had the misfortune of never playing for a winning club in any of his fifteen seasons. Baseball historian Bill James named him one of the ten unluckiest pitchers of all time. With his low ERA, if he had been on good teams, Raffensberger would likely have been a consistent twenty-game winner. How good was he? Well, Hall of Famer Stan Musial named Raffensberger the toughest pitcher he ever faced.

A FLYROD WITH EARS

If there is one Reds pitcher that veteran fans recall as being the most dominating, it is Ewell Blackwell, who pitched for the team in the 1940s and early '50s. Blackwell was a skinny, six-foot, six-inch righthander. One reporter called him a "fly rod with ears." But Blackwell wasn't funny to the hitters. As he pitched, he dipped low and fell off toward the third-base side of the mound as his long right arm whipped the ball toward home plate. To right-handed batters, it looked like Blackwell's pitch was going to wind up in their ear. Blackwell was so intimidating many hitters came up with excuses to take the day off when he was scheduled to pitch. In 1947, no pitcher was better. He won sixteen straight games, including one no-hitter. And Blacky almost duplicated Johnny Vander Meer's back-to-back no-hitter feat in his next start. He took a no-hitter into the ninth inning against the Dodgers. He got the first out, but then gave up a single on a ground ball that went through his legs. Later he said he should have made the play. But to this day, that is the closest anyone has come to the great Vander Meer record.

TEAMMATES CONGRATULATE EWELL BLACKWELL AFTER HIS NO-HITTER ON JUNE 18, 1947.

HIKE, I MEAN STRIKE

The Reds were in a deep slump in the late 1940s and early 1950s. They had eleven straight losing seasons, and 1948 was no exception. The Reds finished dead last in pitching and hitting, and they finished seventh overall in the eight-team league, just one-half game ahead of the last-place Cubs. The season was not without highlights. Hank Sauer, who would later go on to a long career with the Cubs, finished fourth in the league with thirty-five home runs, which was a new club record. His young teammate at first base, Ted Kluszewski, playing his first full season with the Reds in 1948, hit his first major league home run, and he would go on to break Sauer's mark a few years later. Big Klu had played some college football prior to joining the Reds, and maybe the club thought there was more talent hiding in players who played other sports. In 1948, the Reds roster included Frank Baumholtz and Howie Schultz, who both played pro basketball. Schultz, a first baseman, played on two NBA championship teams with the Minneapolis Lakers in 1951 and

BIG TED KLUSZEWSKI, BRINGING THE LUMBER

1952, which is no surprise when you are six-foot, eight-inches tall. And late in the season, the Reds even managed to find an ex-NFL player to add to the lineup. Steve Filipowicz had played linebacker and fullback for the New York Giants in 1945 and 1946. Too bad they couldn't find a few more baseball players.

WALKER COOPER'S BIG DAY

In 1949, a new sporting venue, the Cincinnati Gardens, opened in Cincinnati, and maybe the Reds would have done better playing there. Because Crosley Field was not exactly the friendly confines for the Reds. The Reds were thirty games under .500 and finished thirty-five games out of first place. The one milestone moment during that 1949 season belonged to a catcher named Walker Cooper. Cooper came to the Reds in a trade with the Giants and only appeared in half the Reds games that season. But on July 6 he enjoyed the greatest single-game batting performance in Reds history. Cooper was hot and so was the weather; the thermometer hit ninety-nine degrees that day, but it didn't affect the big catcher. Cooper had six hits, including three home runs, a double, and a single, and drove in ten runs. The ten RBIs in one game is still the club record. Of all the other great Reds sluggers—Ernie Lombardi, Frank Robinson, Ted Kluszewski, George Foster, Johnny Bench, Tony Perez, Ken Griffey, Jr.—none of them had a day like Walker Cooper.

GROUNDS CREW

When the historical highlight of the season belongs to the grounds crew, you know it wasn't much of a year to brag about. In 1950, the Reds grounds crew debuted a ritual that is now very familiar—dragging the diamond at the end of the fifth inning. Soon every other team adopted the practice. As for the action on the well-raked diamond, well, the Reds lost their first six games, and that wasn't their worst losing streak. They lost ten in a row in August. It all added up to a 66-87 record and a sixth-place finish. Thank goodness for Ted Kluszewski and Ewell Blackwell, who provided some star power for the Reds. Blackwell appeared in the All-Star game and earned the victory with three shut-out innings. In his career, Blackwell was an outstanding All-Star pitcher. He appeared in six consecutive All-Star games from 1946 to 1951, which is an All-Star record.

BIG KLU'S RIVAL

Unexpectedly good pitching kept the Reds near .500 for the first half of the '51 season, but a weak offense that wound up last in the league couldn't support the pitching often enough, and the Reds wound up in sixth place. One of the bright spots on offense was first baseman Ted Kluszewski. But another big muscular youngster was also drawing attention in the lineup, outfielder Joe Adcock. Adcock was three years younger than Klu, and in his second season. The two might have been Redleg teammates for several years, but for the fact that Adcock was also a natural first baseman. After the 1952 season, the Reds decided to stick with Klu, and they traded Adcock to Milwaukee. As it turned out, the Reds would have done well keeping Adcock. Joe went on to have a seventeen-year career, and he actually hit ninety-six more home runs than Kluszewski after 1952. But could Joe Adcock ever have achieved the legendary status of Big Klu? Klu went on to set the Reds single-season and career home run records, and with his massive biceps bulging out of his shortened sleeves, he became the poster boy for home runs and power in baseball in the 1950s. You'll see one of Kluszewski's historic uniforms when you visit the Reds Hall of Fame.

REDLEGS IN THE OUTFIELD

Remember the movie *Angels in the Outfield*? It was a Disney release back in 1994, featuring Danny Glover and Tony Danza, about divine intervention that helps the

Angels win the pennant. It was a re-make of a 1951 movie of the same name, starring Paul Douglas and Janet Leigh. Also appearing in cameo roles in the original were Joe DiMaggio, Ralph Kiner, Ty Cobb, and your 1951 Cincinnati Redlegs. The team needing divine intervention in the original version was Pittsburgh, and early in the season, the movie crew came to Forbes Field to record some game action. They happened to pick a game when the Reds were in town. The movie includes several play-by-play scenes involving the Reds. Ewell Blackwell, Ted Kluszewski, and Roy McMillan were among the Redlegs on the field that day.

THE BELLS

Gus Bell came to the Reds in 1951 in a trade from Pittsburgh, a move that the legendary Pirate General Manager Branch Rickey called the worst trade he ever made. Bell, who later made Cincinnati his home, would be considered a five-tool player today. He could hit, hit with power, run, throw, and field with exceptional skill. He

was a four-time All-Star in an era when the center field competition included a couple of guys named Willie Mays and Duke Snider. Bell's contribution to baseball did not stop with his retirement in 1964. His son Buddy and grandsons David and Mike also played in the big leagues, making the Bells a three-generation baseball family.

GUS BELL POSES WITH HIS FAMILY JULY 5, 1960, ON REDS FAMILY NIGHT. FUTURE RED BUDDY BELL IS SECOND FROM THE RIGHT.

JOE COMES HOME

The television set had made its way into more than twenty million homes by 1952, with popular stars like Bob Hope appearing on TV for the first time that year. The Reds appeared occasionally on the new medium, with radio legend Waite Hoyt and Bob Gilmore providing the play-by-play. And that would have been the first year you might have caught a glimpse of Joe Nuxhall on the tube. Eight years after his famous debut at the age of fifteen in 1944, Nuxhall finally made it back to the big show. The well-traveled Nuxhall had toured the minors with stops in Birmingham, Syracuse, Lima, Muncie, Tulsa, Columbia, and Charleston before he rejoined the Reds. Ironically, Nuxhall's big break in the 1952 season happened in one of the worst games the Reds ever played, a 19-1 loss to Brooklyn at Ebbetts Field. Brooklyn set a major league record by scoring fifteen runs in the first inning. The Reds used four pitchers, and the inning lasted fifty-nine minutes! But as it turned out the game had a silver lining. Nuxhall had struggled in the first weeks of the 1952 season, and he later found out Reds management was on the verge of sending him back to the minors. But in this blowout game with seemingly nothing on the line, he pitched the final three innings in relief and shut out the Dodgers. "We were going to send you down," said Gabe Paul, the Reds general manager. "But after what you did against the Dodgers, I changed my mind." A Cincinnati legend had come home.

1952 TEAM PHOTO

On a summer afternoon in 1952, the Reds players gathered at Crosley Field before a game with the Brooklyn Dodgers to take a team photo. Nothing unusual about that, but joining the players on the field were hundreds of front office people, including the ushers and vendors. The photo was the brainchild of *Collier's Magazine*, which wanted to show readers how many people it took to support the twenty-five ballplayers on the field. Three hundred sixty-six people wound up in the photo, including ninety ushers, one hundred vendors, forty-three police officers, and thirty groundskeepers. The photo turned out great; it was spread across two pages of the August 9, 1952, issue. But taking the picture proved a challenge. It was one hundred and five degrees, one of the hottest days in Cincinnati history, and long delays in staging the photo caused irate fans waiting outside to stage a "heated" commotion.

THE OLD LEFT-HANDED SLUGGER

The winner of the Oscar for best movie was *From Here to Eternity*, which certainly could have been the title given to the 1953 Reds season, which to fans probably seemed to last an eternity. The Reds finished twenty games under .500, thirty-seven games out of first place. The one bright spot was Ted Kluszewski. Big Klu ripped forty home runs in 1953, the first of three straight seasons Klu hit over forty, a club record that Adam Dunn tied in 2006. And another Reds slugger emerged in 1953. Pitcher Joe Nuxhall hit his first home run. Joe went on to hit thirteen homers for the Reds in his career, which is still the club record for a pitcher. Maybe we'll have to start calling the Old Lefthander, "the Old Slugger."

A RED BY ANY OTHER NAME

How did the Reds do? Are the Reds on tonight? The Reds—everybody knows the Cincinnati baseball club by its long-time nickname. The only exception to the name "Reds" came during the height of the Cold War in 1953 when the club changed its official name to "Redlegs" because the label "Reds" was often used to refer to our enemies, the communists. But the new nickname only lasted a few years, and by 1960 the club was called the "Reds" again. The name of course, is derived from the red socks the club has worn since the 1860s. When the team first appeared in its new socks, the press had a field day. They called them the "Red Stockings," the "Scarlet Leggings," and my favorite, the "Knights of the Crimson Hose."

THE "NOTHIN' BALL"

Cincinnati has hosted four All-Star Games including 1953, when the National League defeated the American League, 5-1. Gus Bell and Ted Kluszewski were the Reds representatives, but the hitting stars were Enos Slaughter and Pee Wee Reese. There were twenty-one future Hall of Fame players at Crosley Field that day, including Stan Musial, Mickey Mantle, and Jackie Robinson. But the fan's attention was focused on two players, and one wasn't even in uniform. Ted Williams had just returned from a tour of duty in Korea and was limited to throwing out the ceremonial first pitch. The other attraction was a forty-seven-year-old pitcher, Satchell Paige, the legendary Negro League star, who was playing for Kansas City. Paige promised to throw his "nothin' pitch": "It ain't got nothin' on it, and they can't hit it." Paige pitched one inning, becoming the oldest player to ever appear in an All-Star Game.

GUS BELL AND TED KLUSZEWSKI POSE WITH THE NATIONAL LEAGUE'S MANAGER, CHARLIE DRESSEN, BEFORE THE 1953 ALL-STAR GAME.

BREAKING THE COLOR LINE

The Reds finished fifth in 1954, led by Ted Kluszewski's monster year: forty-nine home runs and 141 RBIs. Ted became the first Red to lead the league in home runs and RBIs in the same year. It is one of the ten best seasons ever for a Red. But my favorite Klu stat of that year was his strikeouts: only thirty-five. Think about that for a minute. Forty-nine home runs and thirty-five strikeouts. Fewer strikeouts

Cincinnati Reds

CHUCK HARMON (LEFT) AND NINO ESCALERA (RIGHT) BROKE THE TEAM'S COLOR BARRIER IN 1954.

than home runs, and that wasn't the only year he accomplished that feat. He did it four years in a row. There were other milestones that year, including the integration of the Cincinnati roster. The Reds became the ninth club in baseball to play an African-American, some seven years after Jackie Robinson and the Dodgers had integrated baseball in 1947. Two players of color, Puerto Rican Nino Escalera and African-American Chuck Harmon both debuted in the same game, on April 17, against the Braves in Milwaukee. Escalera played just the 1954 season in the major leagues; Harmon played four years in the majors, including three in Cincinnati. Harmon settled in Cincinnati after his playing days, and the Reds celebrate his historic achievement with a plaque at Great American Ball Park.

TEMPLE'S DRAMATIC HIT

Waite Hoyt, the legendary Reds broadcaster from 1942 to 1965, saw nearly four thousand Cincinnati games in his twenty-four-year career, including no-hitters and the 1961 World Series. But, according to Waite, one of the most dramatic moments came on September 24, 1954, a game that meant absolutely nothing in the pennant race. The game was the completion of a suspended game that due to an appeal by

the Reds had to be replayed starting with two outs and two on in the top of the ninth in Milwaukee with the Reds trailing, 3-1. Johnny Temple, the Reds second baseman for most of the 1950s, was the batter, and his at-bat had been the focus of attention for two days. Could Temple deliver with the game on the line? Hoyt recalled that Temple, "with ice-water in his veins, slammed the first pitch to center for a single that tied the game." Hoyt said at the time that nothing matched Temple's at-bat for sheer drama and suspense.

THE HOT-TEMPERED, SLICK-FIELDING JOHNNY TEMPLE

143

GLOVES ON THE FIELD

Did you know that at one time outfielders and infielders, when an inning was over, left their gloves on the field? The players would toss their gloves onto the grass near their position and then pick them up when they came back on the field the next inning. Although it would seem the gloves might interfere with batted balls, in fact, there are very few stories of balls striking these discarded mitts. However, in 1954, baseball adopted a new rule: no more leaving gloves on the field. Now, players had to take them back to the dugout. One veteran baseball man complained that the new rule was going to make games last longer! He was afraid the players would throw their gloves in the dugout and then wouldn't be able to find them. Sounds like a scene out of *The Bad News Bears*.

READY TO NEGOTIATE

In 1954, an over-capacity crowd of thirty-three thousand fans attended the opener at Crosley Field, and as was the custom on Opening Day, the club put up temporary seats in left and center field to handle the overflow. These seats created the need for special rules: any ball hit into the crowd was a ground-rule double. In the 1954 opener, Jim Greengrass of the Reds took every advantage of the temporary seats, hitting four ground-rule doubles, which tied the major league record for most doubles in a game. Greengrass didn't realize he had set a record, but he knew he had had a very good day, and after the game, Reds general manager Gabe Paul asked his young outfielder how he was feeling. "Ready to negotiate," came the quick reply.

BIRDIE AND THE BOMBERS

Some music historians date 1955 as the birth of rock 'n' roll, with the hit "Rock Around the Clock," by Bill Haley and the Comets. At Crosley Field that year, the

POPULAR MANAGER BIRDIE TEBBETTS GUIDED THE REDS RESURGENCE
IN THE MID-1950S.

fans were dancing to "Birdie and the Bombers." Manager Birdie Tebbetts's offense was second in the league, led by big Ted Kluzewski, Wally Post, and Gus Bell, but the Reds season was stymied by inconsistent pitching. It all added up to a fifth-place finish. It was the kind of season that got the best of manager Tebbetts, who at one point wound up in a brawl with Cardinals manager Harry Walker! Not something you see too often, two managers going at it. Here's what happened. The Reds and Cardinals were tied at Crosley Field in the ninth inning when Tebbetts thought the Cardinals were stalling, hoping the game might be postponed due to threatening weather. He went to home plate to complain. Walker, feeling left out, decided to join the discussion group. Evidently Birdie didn't think Walker was invited, and he

BIRDIE'S BOMBERS (L-R) FRANK ROBINSON, ED BAILEY, WALLY POST, TED KLUSZEWSKI, AND GUS BELL

took a swing at the St. Louis skipper. The two wound up in a wrestling match at home plate. The scuffle cost them an ejection and a hundred-dollar fine.

INFIELD MANUEVERS

Everybody knows the basic defensive positions: three outfielders and six infielders. But there is nothing in the rules that says you have to do it this way. A manager is free to place his defensive players anywhere on the field, and that is just what Reds skipper Birdie Tebbetts did on June 16, 1955, against the Giants in New York. With the game tied in the tenth, and the Giants in an obvious sacrifice situation, Tebbetts devised an unusual defense. He stationed two infielders just feet away from the batter to cut off the bunt and brought in Frank Robinson, his left fielder, to play a normal third base position, leaving just two outfielders. The Giants decided they couldn't bunt against this defense, and their pitcher flew out to center field. And not to be outdone, in another game Tebbetts used four outfielders for one play! Now, you can see a lot of baseball games before you see a play with four outfielders. Wonder what they called that fourth one?

ONE MILLION

Led by rookie Frank Robinson, Ted Kluszewski, Wally Post, Gus Bell, and Ed Bailey, the Redlegs tied the National League team home run record of 221, and to this day that club is recalled as having one of the greatest power lineups in Reds history. But of even more significance for the future of the Reds was another record they set that year. That was the then all-time club attendance mark of 1,125,928. This was the first time the Reds had topped the one million mark, and it happened as the automobile was becoming the major means of travel for most fans. In earlier years, people hopped on the streetcars to reach Crosley Field, but now the automobile was king, and the neighborhood around Crosley became a traffic nightmare.

The narrow streets and alleys and lack of parking lots created baseball gridlock. For a while, there was talk of the club moving out of town, but the city finally cleared land for parking lots, and in the 1960s, put together the deal for the new downtown ballpark, Riverfront Stadium. The big sluggers of 1956 were not only hitting the ball out of the ballpark, they were building a case for a new ballpark too.

VOTE EARLY, VOTE OFTEN

The Reds were picked by some to win the National League pennant in 1957 after their strong third-place finish in 1956. And manager Birdie Tebbetts had his sluggers in first place on July 2, but a second-half pitching collapse doomed the Redlegs to a fourth-place finish, fifteen games behind Hank Aaron and the Milwaukee Braves. That was also the summer of the All-Star voting scandal, when the Reds faithful stuffed the ballot boxes. There were an estimated half-million All-Star ballots cast in the Cincinnati area, more than all the other areas of the country combined. There were so many ballots arriving at the last minute at the offices of the *Cincinnati Times-Star*, which was the Cincinnati paper sponsoring the vote, that the staff couldn't handle the deluge. All eight of the Reds starters in 1957 were ahead in the voting at one point. Reds players edged out some guys named Mays and Musial and Aaron. The commissioner stepped in at the last minute and added those three future Hall of Famers to the team, but the Reds still sent six players: Ed Bailey, Johnny Temple, Roy McMillan, Don Hoak, Frank Robinson, and Gus Bell. Surprisingly, the list didn't include Ted Kluszewski. The popular slugger had suffered a back injury and was a part-time player. He was traded to Pittsburgh after the season.

THE FIRST GOLD-GLOVE SHORTSTOP

In the 1950s, *Sports Illustrated* decided to feature a shortstop on the cover of their magazine, and they turned to everybody's number one candidate, Roy McMillan

ROY McMILLAN WAS CONSIDERED THE FINEST DEFENSIVE SHORTSTOP OF THE 1950S.

of the Reds. The team has had a string of great shortstops since McMillan—Leo Cardenas, Dave Concepcion, Barry Larkin—but old-timers will tell you none was a slicker fielder than little Mac. And how much was he appreciated? In 1956, on a Reds team famed for its home runs, the sports writers, impressed by watching McMillan play short, gave him the team MVP award over his more popular home-run bashing teammates. And McMillan's fame was not limited to Cincinnati. He won the first-ever Gold Glove award for shortstops in 1957.

COMEDY CENTRAL

The second game of a Pirates-Reds doubleheader on June 23, 1957, could have doubled as a comedy sketch. The Pirates thought Reds reliever Raul Sanchez was throwing a spitter, and they began complaining to the umpire. Getting no satisfaction, two of the Pirates, Bob Purkey and Dee Fondy, decided to take more drastic action. Fondy grabbed a water bucket and took it out to Sanchez. During the seventh-inning stretch, Purkey started a rain dance behind home plate that had him tossed from the game. In the ninth inning, Fondy took a pair of sunglasses out to the ump, and he soon joined Purkey in the showers. Sanchez must have enjoyed all the jokes, for he wound up earning the save in the 5-2 Reds win. And Fondy and Purkey? I guess the Reds liked their act, because they both joined the Reds the next season!

STAYING HOME

Rumors of the Reds leaving Cincinnati surface every once in a while, but most of those stories have been nothing but idle threats or rumors. Probably the closest the Reds have ever come to leaving Cincinnati was in the late 1950s. First, the traffic and parking situation at Crosley Field had become so difficult that owner Powel Crosley began lobbying the city for a new park. Then in 1957, the Brooklyn Dodgers and

PRE-GAME TRAFFIC ON DALTON STREET HEADED TO CROSLEY FIELD, 1961.

A PARKING LOT NORTH OF DALTON STREET, JUST SOUTH OF CROSLEY, IS FILLED UP PRIOR TO A TWI-NIGHT DOUBLEHEADER WITH THE CARDINALS, 1961.

the New York Giants announced plans to leave New York for the West Coast. The National League was about to lose its New York teams, and league officials immediately thought of the unhappy Reds to fill the void. Powel Crosley and other club officials flew to New York. Gabe Paul, the Reds general manager, backed the idea of the Reds moving, but Crosley finally vetoed the deal. "I don't want to have to get into my airplane and fly to New York every time I want to see the Reds play," Crosley said, and that was that. The Reds remained in Cincinnati.

THE SEATING AREA IN RIGHT FIELD KNOWN AS THE GOAT RUN WAS ADDED IN FRONT OF THE PERMANENT RIGHT-FIELD BLEACHERS.

GOAT RUNS AND HOME RUNS

The Reds of the 1950s tended to feature power-laden clubs that lacked solid pitching, but 1958 was just the opposite. The Reds finally got good pitching, but the offense struggled. The Reds finished in fourth place, two games under .500. And one of the reasons the pitching improved and the offense slumped was that the club, with the fans support, actually made Crosley Field a bigger ballpark. In 1958, the fans supported the club's decision to increase the distance down the right field line. For most of the 1950s, the Reds had installed a temporary seating area in front of the right field bleachers. This area, which somehow picked up the nickname of the "Goat Run," added a few extra seats and shortened the right field line from 366 feet to 342 feet. With the Goat Run in place, Crosley Field developed quite a reputation as a home run paradise, but club officials decided maybe that was hurting the Reds pitching more than it was helping the club's offense, and in 1958, bolstered in part by a fan survey that called for removing the Goat Run, the club took out the extra seats, and right field returned to its original dimensions of 366 feet. Wouldn't it be interesting to see what the fans would say today given a similar option?

THE LONG SEASON

The price of gas was about twenty-five cents a gallon in 1959, the number one movie was *Ben Hur*, and the hit song was "Smoke Gets in Your Eyes," perhaps a tribute to the Redleg sluggers whose bats were smokin' that season. Despite the bigger dimensions of Crosley field, the Reds offense resumed hitting, led by Frank Robinson and Vada Pinson. But the pitching? Well, it was dead last. The Reds allowed the most runs of any club and it all added up to a fifth-place finish, thirteen games behind the LA Dodgers. One new addition to the club that season was pitcher Jim Brosnan, a native of Cincinnati who went to Elder High School. Brosnan pitched well for the Reds for several years as a starter and reliever, but he is better remembered today for his work with the pen rather than his work out of the 'pen. Brosnan wrote two baseball diaries, *The Long Season*, covering 1959, and *Pennant Race*, which followed the Reds 1961 pennant-winning year. Both are still considered to be baseball classics.

RELIEF PITCHER JIM BROSNAN HELPED THE REDS WIN THE 1961 PENNANT RACE, AND THEN WROTE A BOOK ABOUT IT TITLED *PENNANT RACE*.

FANS ON THE FIELD

Crosley Field holds the distinction of hosting the first night game in major league history, an historic first for the old yard. Crosley also has the distinction of an historic "last." Opening Day 1959 marked the last time fans were allowed to sit on the field for a major league game. This was a practice most teams employed in the early years of baseball, when fields were much larger, and the ball was not as lively. Clubs allowed standing-room-only fans to stand behind ropes in the outfield near the fence. But every team except the Reds had discontinued this practice before 1959. And the Reds only resorted to it on Opening Day. But after the 1959 opener, the Reds announced they, too, would also end this practice, marking the end of a tradition that had lasted since the early days of professional baseball. Not that the pitchers minded. The shortened outfield turned routine outs into easy ground-rule doubles. Phillies pitcher Robin Roberts took one look at the temporary seats on the Crosley Field terrace, and said, "I know how they get rid of those seats after the game. The pitchers go and take them down!"

AWARDS DAY AT CROSLEY FIELD-APRIL, 20, 1969.
SEVERAL REDS WERE HONORED FOR THEIR 1968
ACHIEVEMENTS: (L-R) JOHNNY BENCH (ROOKIE OF THE YEAR),
ALEX JOHNSON (COMEBACK PLAYER OF THE YEAR),
PETE ROSE (BATTING CHAMPION).

THE BUILDING OF
THE MACHINE

1960-1979

DEWITT: ANOTHER LOOK

It may come as a surprise to hear this, but I believe the Reds made one of their best front office moves of all time when they hired Bill DeWitt as their new general manager in 1960. The Reds hired DeWitt after the resignation of Gabe Paul, the Reds long-time GM who left Cincinnati to join the new Houston Colt 45s, or Astros as we know them today. DeWitt is usually remembered by Reds fans as the man who made one of the all-time worst deals in Cincinnati history when he traded Frank Robinson after the 1965 season. But his first trades worked out very well, as he brought in Joey Jay and Gene Freeze and propelled the Reds to the surprise pennant of 1961. And from that point on, the Reds dramatically improved. They had not been a good team under Gabe Paul; their 1960 season was typical, finishing sixth, twenty games under .500. In fact, the Reds had had just two winning seasons in fifteen years before DeWitt took over! He turned the Reds around and kept them there, despite the Robinson deal. The Reds had eight winning seasons in the 1960s, one of their best decades ever. DeWitt's farm system developed Pete Rose and Tony Perez, and his scouts signed Lee May, Johnny Bench, and Gary Nolan, all part of a legacy he left for Bob Howsam and the Big Red Machine.

A CLUB RECORD?

Jim O'Toole, one of the top left-handed pitchers in Reds history, was twenty-three in 1960 when he decided to give up the life of the single ballplayer and get married. O'Toole was from Chicago, and he and his bride scheduled the wedding for a

NEW GENERAL MANAGER BILL DEWITT SHOWS OFF A POSTER OF THE NATIONAL LEAGUE CHAMPION REDS, A TEAM HE HELPED BUILD WITH SHREWD DEALS.

day when the Reds were in the Windy City to play the Cubs. Problem was the wedding date turned out to be the day before O'Toole's regular turn to pitch. Generally, one can assume that getting married the day before you are supposed to start a major league baseball game is not recommended. Manager Fred Hutchinson wasn't happy, but he wouldn't let O'Toole off the hook. "He knew the schedule," growled Hutch. O'Toole started but didn't get out of the fifth inning. Fortunately, his marriage worked out a lot better. Jim and his wife, Betty, have eleven kids, which must be some sort of a club record!

THE MIRACLE RAGAMUFFINS

The memorable 1961 season is best summed up in a couple of nicknames that appeared during the summer of '61—the "Ragamuffin Reds," and the "Miracle on Western Avenue." "Ragamuffin" because the team seemed to have been thrown together at the last minute, with several starters joining the club in off-season deals. And "Miracle on Western Avenue" because this ragamuffin group, playing in Crosley Field on Western Avenue, somehow managed to contend for the pennant. The Reds were picked to finish sixth by most experts, and even the Reds faithful would have been happy with a .500 season. After all, the 1960 Reds had finished twenty games under .500. But the 1961 club surprised everyone by battling the Giants and Dodgers for first place, and after sweeping the Dodgers in a double-header on August 16, before a record crowd of 72,000 at the old Memorial Coliseum in Los Angeles, the Reds were in first place for good, going on to win ninety-three games, an amazing improvement of twenty-six games in one season. "Rally Round the Reds" was their theme song, written by Ruth Lyons and sung daily on her *50-50 Club* television show, but the Reds failed to rally for the last battle, losing to the Yankees in the World Series. Still, the Ragammuffin Reds had truly pulled off a miracle.

THE "OTHER" GUYS

The Yankees handled the Reds pretty easily in the 1961 World Series, winning four games to one. Certainly that New York team was loaded with stars: Mickey Mantle, Roger Maris, Yogi Berra, and Whitey Ford. Yet the Reds pitching held Maris and Mantle to a combined three-for-twenty-five and eight strikeouts. Instead it was the "other" guys who whupped up on the Reds: Bill Skowron, Johnny Blanchard, Bobby Richardson, and Elston Howard. For the Reds, well, it was our "other" guys who had the best series as well. Frank Robinson and Vada Pinson figured to be the offensive stars, but they combined for just five hits in thirty-seven at bats. Instead, it was rookie catcher Johnny Edwards, veteran outfielder Wally

Post, and light-hitting shortstop Eddie Kasko who led the team in hitting. And the highlight play for the Reds? It involved a backup infielder—Elio Chacon—who stunned the Yankees with a surprising run for home in Game Two at Yankee Stadium on a passed ball that had rolled just feet away from catcher Elston Howard. Chacon's mad dash put the Reds ahead, 3-2, and they went on to win Game Two, their only victory in the Series.

(TOP) ELIO CHACON, THE REDS STAR OF GAME TWO IN THE 1961 WORLD SERIES, POINTS TO A FRONT-PAGE DESCRIPTION OF HIS HEROICS; (ABOVE) YANKEE CLETE BOYER DOUBLES TO LEFT OFF JIM BROSNAN IN GAME FOUR OF THE SERIES.

REDS FANS TURN OUT TO
GREET THEIR TEAM, THE
1961 NATIONAL LEAGUE
CHAMPIONS.

CHARGE!

The early 1960s were great years in Cincinnati sports history. The UC Bearcats won the NCAA basketball tournament in 1962 for the second straight season, and the Reds were the defending National League champions. In trying to repeat, the Reds had a great season in 1962. They won ninety-eight games, five more than the year before when they won the pennant, but LA and San Francisco were better, and the Reds finished third. Frank Robinson was in the race for the batting championship until the final days of the season, finishing second to Tommy Davis of the Dodgers. The club tried a couple of interesting promotions that year. The first "Rock 'n' Roll Night" was held at Crosley Field with six local bands twisting the night away. And in August the club staged the first and last "Trumpet Night" promotion. Anyone bringing a trumpet got in free, and some six hundred trumpeters marched into the stands carrying their horns, no doubt ready to entertain the Crosley fans with six hundred different versions of "Charge." Probably all off-key.

FRANK ROBINSON

If a player has one season when he hits .300 with thirty home runs and a hundred RBIs, he has had a great year. That is why Frank Robinson is the greatest hitter in Reds history, for Robinson didn't just have one of those years, he averaged that output for ten years in a row. When he left the Reds after the 1965 season, Robinson held club records for home runs, RBIs, runs scored, and slugging percentage. He won the MVP in 1961, and he should have won it again in 1962. He had a much better year in '62—at one point he hit eleven homers in a twelve-game span—but the award went to LA's Maury Wills. The club retired Robinson's number twenty in 1998, his statue stands on Crosley Terrace at the entrance to Great American Ball Park, and you can see his plaque when you visit the Reds Hall of Fame.

PINSON AND ROBBY

Who has been the best offensive duo in Reds history? You could certainly make a strong case for Johnny Bench and Tony Perez. In their nine seasons together as

starters, Bench and Perez averaged fifty-four home runs, 206 RBIs, and 166 runs scored. But there is another pair of teammates that can stake just as strong a claim: Frank Robinson and Vada Pinson. In their seven seasons together as starters, Robinson and Pinson averaged fifty-two home runs, 198 RBIs, and 210 runs scored. In 1962, Pinson and Robinson directly accounted for over 50 percent of the Reds 802 runs, the most dominating season a pair of Reds has ever had.

VADA PINSON AND FRANK ROBINSON READY THEIR BATS FOR THE OPENING GAME OF THE 1961 WORLD SERIES IN YANKEE STADIUM. DESPITE HAVING GREAT YEARS, BOTH HIT POORLY IN THE SERIES.

THE OTHER JOHNNY

So here's a question that might win you a bet or two. Who was the first Reds catcher to win a Gold Glove? Johnny Bench has ten of them, but he wasn't the first Red. That honor goes to another Johnny—Johnny Edwards, the Reds catcher of the 1960s who was eventually replaced by Bench in 1968. Edwards won Gold Gloves for defensive excellence in 1963 and 1964, and he made three All-Star teams. He grew up in Columbus, Ohio, and debuted with the Reds in 1961 at the age of twenty-three. Although he wasn't the starting catcher that season, he played extensively in the 1961

World Series and wound up hitting .364. Largely forgotten after Bench replaced him, Edwards should be remembered as a fine defensive catcher. Bench led the league in fielding percentage once in his career; Edwards did it four times.

STAN THE MAN

In 1963, parents puzzled over the lyrics to a new pop song, "Louie Louie," and Reds manager Fred Hutchinson puzzled over how to revive his sagging club. Picked by many to contend for the pennant, Hutch's boys struggled that season, finishing fifth. One bright spot for the Reds was young Jim Maloney, who won twenty-three games. In a game against Milwaukee he set a club record with eight consecutive strikeouts. Another bright spot for the Reds was a rookie second baseman, native son Pete Rose, who surprised everyone in the organization by winning the second base job in spring training. Rose won the Rookie of the Year Award in a landslide, hitting .273 and scoring 101 runs. No one at the time imagined he would one day wind up the hit king of baseball. But if you had had a crystal ball on September 29 of that year, you would have realized you were watching the changing of the guard. The Reds played the Cardinals, in what was the last game of Stan Musial's long career. Musial's final hit, which was then the National League hit record of 3,630, was a single that bounded past the young Rose, who eighteen years later would bound past Stan the Man with hit number 3,631 to break Musial's NL record.

CROSLEY WAS NO "COOKIE-CUTTER"

Baseketball floors have a standard size; football fields do too. But one of the great things about baseball parks is how different they are from city to city. In the 1970s, baseball moved away from the old tradition of unique sizes and began using "cookie-cutter" designs, represented here by Riverfront Stadium. The most recent wave of new ballpark construction in the last fifteen years has seen baseball return to the quirky

PETE ROSE SHOWS HIS ROOKIE OF THE YEAR TROPHY TO MANAGER FRED HUTCHINSON.

dimensions of the earlier era. At old Crosley Field, you had the outfield terrace, which was certainly unique, but even the outfield walls had their idiosyncrasies. The center field wall did not line up evenly with the fence in front of the right-field bleachers. It was so confusing the club painted a horizontal line on the wall to help determine when a home run was hit. And even that wasn't enough: in big letters, the Reds painted on the wall: "Batted Ball Hitting Wall to Right of White Line on Fly Home Run." Crosley was such an odd little park the ground rules had to be printed on the walls!

A BITTERSWEET YEAR

The 1964 season was the only time that the Reds lost the National League pennant on the last day of the season. The club had floundered for the first few months of the year with a so-so record, while the Phillies ran off to a big lead. But the Reds stayed close, and in mid-September they had closed to six games behind the Phils. The Reds then won nine in a row while the Phillies collapsed, and heading into the final day of the season, the Reds, Phillies, and Cardinals all had a chance to win or tie for the pen-

nant. The Reds hosted the Phillies at Crosley Field, but the Reds folded early, losing 10-0, while the Cardinals beat the Mets and captured the pennant. As a backstory to all the excitement of the pennant race, Reds manager Fred Hutchinson battled illness. The tough, hard-nosed skipper had been diagnosed with cancer in January but tried to manage the club most of the season. As the weeks wore on, Hutch missed more and more time, and coach Dick Sisler became the acting manager. Six weeks after the season ended, Fred Hutchinson passed away at the age of forty-five. The next season, Hutch was elected to the Reds Hall of Fame, and his number one was officially retired by the club.

FRED HUTCHINSON COMPILED A RECORD OF 443-372 AS SKIPPER OF THE REDS.

SO LONG, WAITE! AND HELLO, JOHNNY!

Nineteen sixty-five was the summer of the Beatles and Motown, and the final year of a popular Crosley Field soundtrack: Announcer Waite Hoyt retired after twenty-three years of broadcasting play by play. And Waite almost had a pennant winner in his final season. The Reds offense was number one in the National League, led by Frank Robinson and Pete Rose and Deron Johnson, but the pitching was uneven,

LEGENDARY REDS RADIO ANNOUNCER SAYS GOODBYE TO FANS AT A FAREWELL CEREMONY IN 1965 AT CROSLEY FIELD.

even though Jim Maloney was the ace of the staff, and Sammy Ellis won twenty-two games. But the staff lacked depth, and the Reds faltered in September to finish fourth, eight games behind the Dodgers. That year also marked the arrival of the first combat troops in Vietnam, and the military draft soon became a controversial issue.

Baseball had its own kind of draft that summer; 1965 was the first year the clubs agreed to a draft of amateur players, and the Reds first choice was a Michigan high school player named Bernie Carbo. Their second-round choice? Another high school player, a seventeen-year-old catcher from Oklahoma named Johnny Lee Bench.

THE FIREBALLER

The most dominating Reds pitcher of the last half-century was Jim Maloney, a big right-hander whose fastball has been estimated at one hundred mph. Maloney was in the same category as Nolan Ryan and Sandy Koufax when it came to sheer speed. And he had the dominating pitching performances to prove it. He threw five one-hitters and three no-hitters, including two that lasted more than nine innings. They both happened in the summer of 1965, just two months apart. In his first extra-inning no-hitter, tied 0-0 in the eleventh against the Mets, Maloney finally gave up a hit and lost the game, 1-0. In his next extra-inning gem, against

REDS TEAMMATES CARRY JIM MALONEY OFF THE FIELD AFTER HIS THIRD NO-HITTER, IN APRIL 1969.

the Cubs in Chicago, the Reds again failed to score in regulation, but finally scored one run in the top of the tenth. Maloney pitched the bottom of the tenth, walked one, but got Ernie Banks to hit into a double play for the final outs.

CHRISTENSEN AND JOHNSON

Sometimes when a young player has a great year, it can cause a club to make moves it might not have considered. In 1926, the Reds had a rookie outfielder named Cuck-oo Christensen who hit .350, which is still the club record for rookies. The Reds thought so highly of him, they decided to trade away veteran center fielder Edd Roush. Oops, big mistake: Christensen hit only .250 the next year in what proved to be his last year in the majors. Roush went on to have several more good seasons. Jump forward to 1965, when twenty-six-year-old Deron Johnson knocked in 130 runs. His success made Frank Robinson expendable, and soon Robinson was on his way to Baltimore. Oops, another big mistake: Robinson went on to win the triple crown in Baltimore. Johnson struggled to fill Robinson's shoes and never again had a great season.

FROM ROBINSON TO CARROLL....

Milt Pappas, Jack Baldschun and Dick Simpson. They are the answer to a Reds trivia question that no one really likes to remember: Who did the Reds get for Frank Robinson in the infamous 1965 trade with Baltimore? Pappas, a starting pitcher, Baldschun, a reliever, and Simpson, a young outfielder, failed to last long in Cincinnati. Baldschun and Simpson were gone in just two years, and Pappas was traded to Atlanta in the middle of the 1968 season. So the Robinson deal was a disaster? Well, not entirely. Pappas was traded for three players, including a pitcher who went on to become one of the stars of the Big Red Machine and who ranks third on the Reds all-time save list: Clay Carroll. In the chain of events, Robinson became Pappas, and Pappas became Carroll. So there was something salvaged from the infamous Robinson deal, after all.

THE TRADE THAT WILL LIVE IN INFAMY: (TOP) FRANK ROBINSON SWINGS FOR
THE FENCES; (LOWER LEFT): MILT PAPPAS, JACK BALDSCHUN, AND DICK SIMPSON; (LOWER
RIGHT) CLAY "THE HAWK" CARROLL, WHO GAVE A SILVER LINING TO THE DARK CLOUD.

A VERY LONG RAIN DELAY

The 1966 version of the Reds had one of the worst records of the decade. They finished in seventh place, and perhaps fans knew the season was lost even before it started. For the first time in the twentieth century, rain forced the team to open on the road. The Reds were scheduled for a three-game series with the Mets to start the season, but rain postponed the opener not once, not twice, but for the entire three-game series. The Reds wound up opening in Philadelphia, where, without parades and hoopla, they lost, 4-3. The home opener was finally held eleven days late on April 22, which, for you Reds trivia buffs, was the first time the home opener was played at night. And another bit of trivia from the final day of the season: On October 2, Joe Nuxhall played his last game, pitching a third of an inning against the Atlanta Braves.

FOUR CONSECUTIVE HOME RUNS

Of the hundreds of Reds games I listened to as a fan growing up in the 1950s and '60s, I can still recall the night game of August 12, 1966, at Crosley Field when Art Shamsky, a reserve outfielder, pinch hit late in the game and smacked a home run. The game went into extra innings, and Shamsky hit two more homers in his next two at-bats, giving him three in a row. The Reds finally lost the game, 14-11, but Shamsky's homer string had everyone wondering if he could hit one in his next at-bat for a record-tying four in a row. Despite his hot bat, manager Don Heffner didn't play him the next day. He didn't start the next game either, but he was called on to pinch hit in the seventh inning, and facing Vernon Law of the Pirates, Shamsky drilled another home run. That tied the major league record of four home runs in four consecutive at-bats. The only other Red to accomplish that feat was Johnny Bench, who also did it over two games in 1973. Bench hit one on May 8 in his last at-bat in a game against the Phillies, and the next day, facing Hall-of-Famer Steve Carlton, Bench homered three times.

ROOKIES ON THE FIELD; VETS IN THE BOOTH

The beginnings of the Big Red Machine could be seen stirring in the Cincinnati line-up in 1967. Nobody used that nickname yet. After all, the Reds teams of the late 1960s did not win a pennant, but the lineup in 1967 featured Pete Rose, Tony Perez, Vada Pinson, and Tommy Helms, along with a few rookies—Lee May, Johnny Bench, and Gary Nolan. May won the *Sporting News* Rookie Player of the Year Award. Nolan made the team out of spring training, at the age of eighteen, after just one year in the minors. Bench debuted at the ripe old age of nineteen late in the season. The 1967 Reds spent fifty-seven days in first place, before a late-season swoon landed them in fourth. The Reds played their longest game in history that season, a twenty-one-inning affair against the Giants at Crosley Field. The game was scoreless until the top of the twenty-first, when Reds pitcher Bob Lee walked Dick Groat with the bases loaded. Gaylord Perry pitched sixteen scoreless innings for the Giants. The game lasted five hours and forty minutes. Bench, just three days after his major league debut, started and caught the entire game. And up in the Crosley radio booth, Joe Nuxhall called the game in his first season as a Reds announcer.

RETIRED PITCHER JOE NUXHALL BEGINS A NEW REDS RADIO TRADITION IN 1967. (L-R): THE NOT-SO-OLD LEFTHANDER, CLAUDE SULLIVAN, AND JIM McINTYRE

TRIPLE PLAY

Ever seen a triple play? How about a "walk-off" triple play! There have been only a handful of triple plays in Reds history, but one of the most memorable was on

A GAME-ENDING TRIPLE PLAY!

May 30, 1967, when the Reds pulled off not just a triple play, but a game-ending triple play. Down 2-1 in the ninth, the Cardinals rallied by putting their first two batters on. Then a ground ball to shortstop started a double play. Hoping to catch the Reds napping, Orlando Cepeda tried to score from third as the second out was made at first base. But Reds first baseman Deron Johnson fired the ball to catcher Johnny Edwards who tagged out Cepeda at the plate. This is the only time in Reds history the final out of the game was made on a triple play.

A TOPSY-TURY SEASON

Nineteen sixty-eight was the year of discontent in America, the assassinations of Robert Kennedy and Martin Luther King, the anti-Vietnam War protests, and the emergence of the counter-culture. The youth movement featured the long-haired "hippy" look, but not in Cincinnati. The clean-shaven Reds even sported a new clean-shaven logo. The club had featured a baseball cartoon character with a mustache since the early 1950s, but new general manager Bob Howsam, who had a rule about no facial hair, decided his club logo needed a shave too. And so the Reds debuted a new Mr. Red in 1968, one without a mustache. In baseball history, 1968 is often called the "Year of the Pitcher" since pitching dominated the game that season. But Cincinnati didn't seem to get the message. Led by Pete Rose and rookie Johnny Bench, the 1968 Reds led the league in batting average and runs scored, but unfortunately, the Reds pitching staff also didn't get the word on the pitching revolution. While the ERA of most clubs dropped sharply, the Reds finished with an ERA half a run higher than the rest of the league. It all added up to a fourth-place finish.

FIREMAN OF THE YEAR

He was the first pure relief pitcher selected to the Reds Hall of Fame. He combined a sidearm motion with a devastating sinker ball. His name: Wayne Granger. Granger came to the Reds from the Cardinals in 1968 along with Bobby Tolan in a trade for Vada Pinson. In 1969, Granger set a major league record for most games for a pitcher, appearing in ninety. He saved twenty-seven games and won nine, along with winning his first Fireman of the Year award. The next year he set the National League save record with thirty-five and took home his second award, becoming the first NL pitcher to win it twice in a row. You can learn more about Wayne Granger and other Reds relievers when you visit the Hall of Fame.

THE BIRTH OF THE MACHINE

The year of 1969 produced some memorable pieces of cultural history: the Woodstock music festival, and the famous movie pairing of Paul Newman and Robert Redford in *Butch Cassidy and the Sundance Kid*. At Crosley Field, the Reds were beginning to make some history as well. Led by Pete Rose, Tony Perez, Lee May, and Johnny Bench, the Reds led the National League in nearly every offensive category, but what was truly memorable was the birth of one of the most famous baseball nicknames of all time. Halfway through the season, the famous "Big Red Machine" nickname first appeared in print. And it wasn't in Cincinnati. Los Angeles sportswriter Bob Hunter used the phrase in a story about a Dodgers-Reds game. By 1970, the Reds media and marketing departments had endorsed it, and it appeared in a Reds publication for the first time.

PETE ROSE BANGS THE THIRD PITCH OF THE 1969 SEASON FOR A HOME RUN. TROTTING TO THE DUGOUT, HE IS CONGRATULATED BY (L-R) ALEX JOHNSON, WOODY WOODWARD, TONY PEREZ, JOHNNY BENCH, TRAINER BILL COOPER, AND TED SAVAGE

WHAT IF?

It is always fun to play "What If," and one of the most interesting "What Ifs" in Reds history is what would have happened had the 1969 Reds won the Western Division. Manager Dave Bristol had the Reds in first place as late as September 12

THE 1969 REDS LED THE NATIONAL LEAGUE IN RUNS SCORED AND HOME RUNS, EARNING THE NICKNAME "THE BIG RED MACHINE." HERE THEY POSE FOR A PHOTO AT CROSLEY FIELD. (L-R): TOMMY HELMS, JOHNNY BENCH, LEE MAY, TONY PEREZ, PETE ROSE, BOBBY TOLAN, AND DARRYL CHANEY

before a sore-armed pitching staff finally gave way, and the Reds slipped out of the race, finishing third, a mere four games behind the Atlanta Braves. Bristol had managed the Reds since 1966 and had led the club to three straight winning seasons. Not a bad record, but Bob Howsam, the Reds president and general manager, wanted to make a change. He picked another young manager, the relatively unknown Sparky Anderson. It turned out to be one of the best personnel moves Howsam ever made. And an obvious one in hindsight. But one has to wonder what Howsam would have done if Bristol had led the Reds into the playoffs in 1969. It would have been a little harder to fire a manager who had just won a division title. Bristol went on to manage Milwaukee, Atlanta, and San Francisco in the 1970s and never had another winning season. As for Sparky, he inherited the foundation of a great team and immediately produced a pennant winner in 1970. He eventually became the first manager to win a World Series in both leagues. Hard to second-guess that decision, even in a game of "What If."

NEW REDS MANAGER SPARKY ANDERSON POSES WITH MONTREAL MANAGER
GENE MAUCH IN 1970.

A YEAR FULL OF HIGHLIGHTS

When you play .700 baseball for one hundred games, you are going to have a very good season, and the Reds did just that in 1970, getting off to a fantastic start under new manager Sparky Anderson. The Reds won seventy of their one hundred games, jumped out to a huge lead and won the division by fourteen and one-half games. There were so many highlights that year we would need an hour on the Reds pre-game show, not just a minute. There was the stardom of Johnny Bench who won the MVP at age twenty-two; there was the closing of Crosley Field on June 24, the opening of Riverfront Stadium on June 30, and the All-Star Game on July 14. The night before the game, Pete Rose and Ray Fosse, the American League All-Star catcher had dinner together. The next night, they met again-at home plate in a jarring collision in the bottom of the twelfth inning. Rose scored the winning run, and Fosse suffered a serious shoulder injury trying to block the plate. It was one of the most dramatic moments in All-Star history and helped cement the image of Rose as a hard-nosed player, the kind of guy who would later admit, "I'd walk through hell in a gasoline suit to play baseball."

NO PITCHIN'

"Get an early lead" is a mantra that every manager could live by. But if ever there was a time when that strategy backfired, it was the 1970 World Series. The Reds faced Baltimore, and the Orioles were favored, in part due to the Reds depleted pitching. Rookie starter Wayne Simpson was lost for the season, starters Jim Merritt and Jim McGlothlin both had sore arms, and Anderson's bullpen was not that deep. The Orioles, on the other hand, had a healthy and tested rotation of Jim Palmer, Mike Cuellar, and Dave McNally. And of course, there were a couple of guys named Robinson, Frank and Brooks. All the attention was on Frank, the ex-Red, at the start of the Series, but Brooks soon stole the spotlight with one of the most spectacular all-around performances in World Series history. Nonetheless, the Reds, coming off their best season in club history, were the Big Red Machine, and they attacked early, taking the lead in four of the five games. Lee May led the offense, knocking in eight runs in the five games, still a World Series record. Yet the pitching was too beat up to protect the leads. The Orioles wound up outscoring the Reds thirty-three runs to twenty, and the Reds team ERA was an awful 6.70. "We just didn't have any pitchin' left," said Sparky. "Nothin', no pitching at all."

BERNIE CARBO SLIDES HOME IN GAME ONE OF THE 1970 WORLD SERIES.
BALTIMORE CATCHER ELROD HENDRICKS APPLIES THE TAG, SANS BASEBALL.
UMPIRE KEN BURKHART, HIS BACK OBVIOUSLY TO THE PLAY, MAKES THE
CONTROVERSIAL CALL: "OUT!"

A ROSE IN CENTERFIELD?

The Reds were the reigning National League champions in 1971, and everyone picked them to repeat. But the troubles for the Reds started early, when in January, at a charity basketball event, Reds centerfielder Bobby Tolan tore his Achilles tendon. He had surgery and hoped to return to the lineup early in the season, but re-injured the tendon in May and missed the entire year. This left the Reds with quite

**FLEET CENTERFIELDER
CESAR GERONIMO**

a problem: They did not have another true centerfielder. Manager Sparky Anderson wound up starting seven different players in center, including Dave Concepcion and Pete Rose. But the Tolan injury became an opportunity for GM Bob Howsam. Early in the season he traded for George Foster, who added depth to the outfield, and after the season, he made the big trade with Houston, sending Tommy Helms and Lee May to the Astros for Joe Morgan, Jack Billingham, and others. But the key to the trade for Howsam was the young center-fielder in the deal, Cesar Geronimo. So Tolan's injury, which looked devastating at the time, and in fact it played a major role in the Reds dismal fourth-place finish that year, wound up bringing the Reds Foster and Geronimo, two of the stars of the Big Red Machine.

THE OTHER TRADE

Any talk of the building of the Big Red Machine always includes the great trade with Houston after the 1971 season that brought Joe Morgan to the Reds. But what about that other trade? The one for George Foster? In the history of the Reds, this has to rank as one of the best five trades of all time. In 1971, Foster was twenty-two with raw power and potential but he was sitting on the Giants bench not getting much playing time. He was prone to striking out, and the Giants, rich in other outfield prospects, and needing middle infielders, agreed to trade Foster to the Reds for backup shortstop Frank Duffy and minor league pitcher Vern Geishert. Although he struggled in his first years with the Reds, by 1975 Foster emerged as one of the hitting stars of the Big Red Machine. For two inconsequential players, the Reds wound up with a National League MVP and a five-time All Star. Interestingly, had the Giants asked another of their outfielders for his opinion, the Giants wouldn't have made the deal. Foster's "going to be some kind of player," said Willie Mays. And Mays was right.

REDS SLUGGERS YOUNG AND OLD: HITTING COACH TED KLUSZEWSKI AND RISING STAR GEORGE FOSTER

MAYBE THAT ASTROTURF WASN'T SO BAD

Astroturf invaded major league baseball parks in the 1960s and 1970s in part because the plastic turf was easier and cheaper to maintain than natural grass. But for Bob Howsam, the Reds general manager when Riverfront Stadium opened, Astroturf wasn't just a budget issue, it was an offensive weapon. He knew the ball moved faster on the turf than it did on grass, and if he had speed in his lineup, he could use the new field to his advantage. Howsam drafted players based on speed—Ken Griffey, Sr., for example, was picked primarily because he was the fastest player the Reds clocked in tryouts. Howsam traded for Joe Morgan, Cesar Geronimo, and George Foster in part because they had speed. Without Astroturf, the Big Red Machine as we know it might never have existed. So the next time you visit the Reds Hall of Fame, give that patch of Astroturf on display a little love pat. It deserves it.

THE PERFECT ASTROTURF SHORTSTOP

Dave Concepcion was selected to nine All-Star teams, won five Gold Gloves, and is certainly one of the top twenty-five shortstops of all time. And so, it is hard to

DAVE CONCEPCION

recall now just how uncertain his future was when he was first signed out of Venezuela in 1968. He was so skinny that Sparky Anderson called him a "little fawn." Pete Rose took one look at the new shortstop and said "You don't have to worry about pulling a muscle. You're so skinny, you'll pull a bone!" Defensively, however, Concepcion was a natural, with great range and a cannon of an arm, a perfect Astroturf shortstop. He took advantage of the surface on his long throws by deliberately throwing the ball on one bounce to first base because he knew he would always get a true hop. Is he a Hall of Famer? Well, Concepcion's not in Cooperstown yet, but you can see his plaque in the Reds Hall of Fame the next time you visit Great American Ball Park.

BACK FROM THE DL: MRS. BENCH

The Reds dominated the National League in 1972. Joe Morgan led the league in runs scored. Pete Rose led the league in hits. Gary Nolan led the league in winning percentage, and the Big Red Machine romped to the Western Division title. The Reds young catcher, twenty-four-year-old Johnny Bench, won his second MVP award and led the league in home runs and RBIs. And he led the league in appearances on the *This Is Your Life* TV show. Hosted by long-time TV personality Ralph Edwards, the show was a sort of surprise family reunion. Bench was the honored guest on the show after a Reds game at Riverfront on September 16. He was brought to home plate after the game and surprised by friends and family members, including his mother who was still a little woozy after being hit in the head by a foul ball. She was hit in the seventh inning and taken to the first aid stand, but recovered in time to make her appearance. Talk about your clutch performances.

A DRAMATIC POST-SEASON

The 1972 post-season should be remembered as one of the best of all-time, with the Reds downing Pittsburgh in a great five-game playoff series before losing to Oakland in a tense seven-game series that featured outstanding pitching and six one-run games. There were so many memorable plays, and it all ended with the sight of Oakland's owner, Charlie Finley, dancing on top of the A's dugout after the Game Seven victory in Cincinnati. But even if the Reds had won, they would have had a hard time topping the dramatic end to the final game against Pittsburgh in the playoffs. It was the fifth game, the game to decide the National League pennant, and the Pirates held a 3-2 lead going into the bottom of the ninth. The Pirates ace reliever, Dave Guisti, was on the mound, but he had to face Johnny Bench to start the inning. With two strikes on him, Bench launched a home run to right field to tie the game, and minutes later, pinch runner George Foster scored the winning run on a wild pitch. Ironically, this game, which many would rate as the most dramatic in Reds history, proved to be historic for another reason: It was the final game in the eighteen-year career of Pirate great Roberto Clemente. The thirty-seven-year-old Clemente died that off-season in a plane crash while delivering aid to earthquake victims in Nicaragua.

JOHNNY BENCH TAGS OUT JOHN "BLUE MOON" ODOM TO END GAME FIVE
OF THE 1972 WORLD SERIES.

"CHICKEN DELIGHT"

Game Sevens are always nail-biting affairs, but someone in the Reds press box during Game Seven of the 1972 World Series found a way to relieve the tension. A member of the media discovered the number of the direct line to Commissioner Bowie Kuhn, who was sitting in the VIP section, and decided to have some fun. The phone rang by Kuhn's seat, and when the commissioner answered he heard the caller ask: "Hello, is this Chicken Delight? I want to order carryout." Kuhn politely informed the caller he had the wrong number. But the press was not to be deterred. Another call: "Hello, Chicken Delight? I want the large size. Twenty-four pieces." By now, Kuhn was not amused. "This isn't Chicken Delight!" he yelled and slammed down the phone. The joke finally wore off, and the practical joker in the press box allowed the commissioner to watch the rest of the game uninterrupted.

BLACK SHOES

In the 1970s, the Reds were known for their conservative, traditional look: short hair, no mustaches or beards, uniforms worn just so. Reds GM Bob Howsam enforced the rules, down to the color of the players' shoes, which had to be black. The Oakland A's began wearing all white shoes in the early '70s, and Howsam hated the look. He thought the all-white shoes made the players' feet look too big, like over-sized clown feet. And he thought that any white on the shoes detracted from the flight of the ball. "The baseball should be the center of attention," said Howsam. Many shoe companies started placing a design on their spikes, and usually it was white. When new shoes arrived in the Reds clubhouse, the clubhouse boys painted over the offensive white markings with black shoe polish.

INTENTIONAL WALKS

You just never know when a memorable moment is going to occur in a baseball game, even during something as ordinary as an intentional walk. On May 16, 1972, the Giants ordered an intentional pass to Pete Rose in the eighth inning with the game tied and a runner on third. The count went to 3-0 when Ron Bryant put ball four too close to the plate. Pete reached out and smacked it into left field for a single to drive in what proved to be the winning run. One of the most famous intentional walk stories is from the 1972 World Series, Game Three, when with the count 3-2 on Johnny Bench, Oakland manager Dick Williams suddenly burst from the dugout waving four fingers and pointing to first base. But it was a trick. He ordered Rollie Fingers to throw a strike and Fingers snuck a perfect low-and-away slider past Bench for strike three. Bench said later he thought something was up and was prepared to swing, but Fingers just threw a perfect pitch.

CARROLL AND BORBON

Remember the nickname Sparky Anderson earned in the 1970s: Captain Hook? He got it for "hooking" his starting pitchers early and turning to his bullpen. You can credit Pedro Borbon and Clay Carroll, the core of the Reds bullpen in the early '70s, with making it possible for Captain Hook to turn to his relief corps so often. Carroll and Borbon both possessed "rubber arms." Sparky could use them nearly every day and pitch them more than one inning. From 1972 to 1978, Borbon averaged seventy appearances a year. And even that wasn't enough. In the "off season," Borbon pitched as a starter in his native Domincan Republic.

KING FOR A DAY

Archie Bunker and the *All in the Family* show ranked number one on TV in 1973, but in Cincinnati Hal King was the number one star of the year. For this was the

UNLIKELY HERO HAL KING HEADS FOR THE PLATE AFTER HIS GAME-WINNING HOME RUN.

189

season when the obscure back-up catcher had the biggest pinch-hit in Reds history. Favored to repeat as NL champs, the Reds found themselves struggling in the first half of the season, falling eleven games behind the Dodgers. And on July 1, when the Reds faced Los Angeles at Riverfront, they were about to fall twelve games behind their arch-rivals. Cincinnati trailed three to one in the bottom of the ninth when Sparky Anderson called on King to pinch hit, with two on and two out. They badly needed a three-run homer to win, and that is exactly what King delivered, a stunning blast off Don Sutton that turned the season around. King had resurrected the Big Red Machine. From that point on, the Reds went fifty-nine and twenty-six, a winning percentage of .694, and won the division by three and a half games over LA.

MOB SCENE

PETE ROSE CIRCLES THE BASES AFTER HITTING THE GO-AHEAD HOME RUN IN THE FOURTH GAME OF THE 1973 NCLS.

One of the scariest moments that Reds players ever faced on the field came at the conclusion of the 1973 NLCS when the Reds were defeated by the Mets in New York. The series was hard-fought; this was the NLCS in which Pete Rose and Bud Harrelson mixed it up at second base, and the Mets fans were eager for revenge. The Mets took a commanding lead late in the final game, and in anticipation of the victory, fans began moving down to the lower box seats. They taunted the Reds fans in the crowd, and the game was delayed at the beginning of the ninth to let the players' families escape to the safety of the clubhouse. At the conclusion of the game, the crowd broke through the police lines, and some five thousand people swarmed the field. Rose, who had been on first base when the final out was made, raced to the Reds dugout, where teammates waited on the top step with bats in hand, in case they needed to protect him.

RIVALS

The Big Red Machine won ninety-eight games in 1974 but finished second, a disappointing year for the team, particularly for Sparky Anderson, because the Reds finished second to the Dodgers. Sparky hated losing to LA, the club that had first signed him as a player. Sparky lived in Southern California, where he had grown up, and his parents often came to see their son when the Reds played the Dodgers. But they knew better than to hang around afterward if the Reds lost. Sparky was in no mood to talk to anybody after losing to the boys in blue. And they lost too often to the Dodgers in 1974—twelve of the eighteen games the clubs played. The Reds closed to within a game and a half in late September and then collapsed, losing six of their next eight, finishing four games back. In the 1970s, these two teams staged one of the great rivalries of all time. They both had Hall of Fame managers, Sparky and Tommy Lasorda, and stable lineups. The Dodger's infield of Steve Garvey, Bill Russell, Davey Lopes, and Ron Cey was almost as well known to Reds fans as their own. They were the two best teams in baseball in the '70s, a fierce rivalry Reds fans still have respect for thirty years later.

MARTY COMES TO CINCINNATI

In 1973, Al Michaels left the Reds broadcast team to do play by play for the Giants. It fell to Assistant GM Dick Wagner to conduct a search for a new broadcaster. Wagner soon found himself listening to a couple of dozen audition tapes. How was he going to decide? There was no scientific test, nor any sophisticated

MARTY BRENNAMAN JOINED JOE NUXHALL IN THE RADIO BOOTH IN 1974.

polling. Wagner listened to a tape, and if the announcer grated on his nerves, he put that tape aside. It all came down to who was the easiest to listen to, and Wagner finally picked a young announcer who was calling play by play for a Triple A team in Virginia, and the Virginia Squires of the old American Basketball Association. Although Dick Wagner turned out to be one of the most unpopular general mangers in Reds history, fans should give him credit for selecting one Hall of Famer—the young announcer Marty Brennaman.

WHO'S ON THIRD?

The powerful Big Red Machine had something to prove in 1975. Recognized as one of the best teams in the NL in the early 1970s, the Reds had had great success but had yet to win a World Series. And third base was one of the big problems facing

Bob Howsam and the Reds front office. Prior to the 1975 season, there were rumors the Reds were planning a big trade, shopping Tony Perez for a third baseman and installing Dan Driessen at first. The trade talks fizzled, and that might be one of the best moves the Reds never made. But when the 1975 season started, the Reds still had not solved their third base problem. The starter was John Vukovich, a good-glove, no-hit utility player. But Sparky's patience grew thin when Vukovich and the Reds got off to a very slow start. On May 3, he inserted a new name at third base: Pete Rose. Rose, who had come up as an infielder, had been playing the outfield since 1967. Pete didn't want to embarrass himself, and he took hundreds of extra ground balls in fielding practice. His teammates never let him forget he wasn't a natural third baseman. Tony Perez yelled over from first base: "Come on, Pete, you need a bulletproof vest!" Joe Morgan was just as quick with an insult: "You can't run, you can't throw, you can't catch!" Rose, who embraced the challenge, responded: "Just watch. I'll be an All-Star at third base." And he was. Not only that, but his move sparked a resurgence of the Big Red Machine. Beginning on May 17, the Reds won sixty-four of their next eighty-four games and won the division going away.

IT'S THE HEAT, NOT THE FEAT

Today, a complete game is something of a rarity, and one can thank Reds manager Sparky Anderson in part, because of his use of his deep bullpen in the 1970s. He pulled pitchers early, and turned it over to his talented relievers. But the lack of complete games was still a novelty then, and during the 1975 season, when the Reds went forty-five games without a starter going the distance, the issue grew and grew in the press as the streak progressed. Finally, Pat Darcy broke the streak with a complete game on a hot, humid night at Riverfront. After the game, a reporter congratulated Darcy and told him people were fainting in the stands. "Over a complete game?" Darcy asked incredulously. The reporter admitted it was the heat and not the feat of the complete game, but Darcy could be excused for thinking his accomplishment had them swooning in the aisles.

1975 WORLD SERIES

Even after some memorable World Series in recent years, the 1975 contest between Cincinnati and Boston remains one of the greatest of all time, highlighted, of course by famous Game Six, won by the Carlton Fisk home run in the bottom of the twelfth inning. Somewhat overlooked in all the heroics was the amazing comeback of the Reds to win the Series the next night. After losing a dramatic extra-inning game in demoralizing fashion, the Big Red Machine might have been on the verge of a collapse. The Reds were on the road in front of the rabid Boston fans, and they fell behind, 3-0, in the third inning. It looked grim until the sixth inning when Tony Perez hit a two-run homer, and the Reds finally took the lead in the ninth. A great comeback in a situation that truly tested the heart of the Big Red Machine.

THE REDS CELEBRATE THE 1975 WORLD SERIES VICTORY OVER THE RED SOX.
(L-R): TONY PEREZ, JOE MORGAN, CLAY CARROLL, JOHNNY BENCH, AND BATTING
PRACTICE COACH ART SEIFERT

A SLIDE AND A HOMER

It took the back-to-back titles of 1975 and 1976 to ensure the Big Red Machine's place in history. And without that first championship in 1975, it is possible we would remember that team as under-achievers instead of one of the greatest teams of all time. The dramatic comeback for the Reds in Game Seven of the 1975 World Series was the biggest victory in club history. Let's take a closer look at the sixth-inning rally that helped turn the game around. The Reds trailed Boston, 3-0, when Pete Rose reached first. With one out Johnny Bench hit what looked like a perfect double-play ball. Not surprisingly, Pete was charging all the way to second, and he slide hard into second baseman Denny Doyle, altering the throw to first. Bench was safe, and that allowed Tony Perez to come up with two outs. Boston pitcher Bill Lee tried to fool Tony with a blooper pitch, but Perez sent it soaring over the Green Monster in left field, and the Reds had closed the gap to one run. That homer turned the momentum, and the Reds eventually won, 4-3. The slide by Rose, and the home run by Perez: When you think about it, has there ever been a rally that was more important to the Reds?

JACK BILLINGHAM WAS THE WORKHORSE OF THE BIG RED MACHINE'S PITCHING STAFF, AVERAGING FIFTEEN VICTORIES FROM 1972 TO 1976.

THAT UNDER-RATED PITCHING STAFF

Nineteen seventy-six is one of the magical years in Reds history, the year the Big Red Machine won 102 games and solidified itself as one of the greatest teams in baseball history, with its sweep of the playoffs and the World Series, winning its second championship in a row, the only National League team to win consecutive World Series since the 1920s. The offense gets all the glory, and well it should because that starting lineup is arguably the best of all time. But let's give the pitching its due. The starters were Gary Nolan, Don Gullett, Jack Billingham, Fred Norman, and Pat Zachry, who won Rookie of the Year honors in 1976. The bullpen boasted Clay Carroll, Pedro Borbon, Rawley Eastwick, and Will McEnaney. No Cooperstown Hall of Famers, no twenty-game winners, but when you factor in the depth and the bullpen, well, as pitcher Pat Darcy said, "Top to bottom, our staff would beat any other. LA might have had three better starters, but our ten-man staff matched up against anybody." So here's to 1976, the glory of the Big Red Machine, and a special tip of the cap to that under-rated pitching staff

WIN IN SEVEN

The 1976 post-season featured, for the first and only time so far, two teams in an NLCS playoff that had both won over one hundred games during the regular season: The Phillies (winners of 101 games) and the Reds (winners of 108). The Reds swept the Phillies in three games—although the third game was another nail-biter, another classic come-from-behind win for the Big Red Machine. The Reds trailed by two runs in the bottom of the ninth before back-to-back home runs by Bench and Foster tied the game, and Griffey won it with an infield single. On the eve of the World Series with New York, the Reds were confident, even brash and cocky. But Sparky was diplomatic. When asked about the World Series, he seemed to give the Yankees their due when he said he thought the Reds would win in seven. The Reds, of course, swept the Yankees in four straight, led by Series MVP Johnny Bench. And only later did Sparky admit he thought the Reds would sweep. His comment about seven games? He had meant that he thought the Reds would wrap up the entire post-season in seven games, and he was right. It is still the only time a team has swept both the playoffs and the World Series. Another tribute to the greatness of the Big Red Machine.

JOHNNY BENCH IS GREETED AT HOME PLATE BY CESAR GERONIMO, DANNY DRIESSEN, AND TONY PEREZ AFTER HITTING HIS SECOND HOME RUN IN GAME FOUR OF THE 1976 WORLD SERIES.

WOULD YOU BELIEVE 128-34?

When you think of the Big Red Machine, you think of that great starting lineup of Rose, Griffey, Morgan, Bench, Perez, Foster, Concepcion, and Geronimo. But how many times did this group actually play together? Well, surprisingly, they played less than one full season as a starting unit. Griffey and Foster did not emerge as starters until 1975, and Perez was traded after the 1976 season. And the big leads the club enjoyed both seasons allowed manager Sparky Anderson to rest his regulars often. This "Great Eight" lineup started as a unit only eighty-seven times in 1975 and 1976, including all the post-season games. Perhaps it was only merciful that Sparky didn't start this line-up together more often. In those eighty-seven games, the "Great Eight" won sixty-nine times and lost eighteen. Projected over a full season that comes to 128-34.

THE GREAT EIGHT: BENCH, GRIFFEY, ROSE, MORGAN, PEREZ, FOSTER, GERONIMO, AND CONCEPCION

THE REAL MR. OCTOBER

Reggie Jackson earned the nickname "Mr. October" for his home-run heroics in the 1977 and 1978 World Series. But as impressive as Jackson's long-ball binge was, it did not compare with the clutch hitting of Johnny Bench in post-season play. He had five dramatic post-season hits in the Reds' final at-bat. In the 1972 playoffs, he homered to tie the fifth and final game in the bottom of the ninth. In the 1973 playoffs against the Mets, he hit a walk-off home run against Tom Seaver to win Game One. In the 1975 World Series against Boston, he started the winning come-from-behind rally in the bottom of the ninth in

Game Two with a double. In the 1976 playoffs versus the Phillies, Bench homered in the bottom of the ninth of Game Three to tie the score at 6-6. And in the top of the ninth inning in Game Four of the 1976 World Series, with the Reds holding a slim 3-2 lead, Bench homered to ice the victory and the sweep of the Yankees. Who is the real Mr. October?? There's no question in Reds country: Johnny Bench.

OK, EVERYBODY INTO THE CLUBHOUSE!

When the final out of the World Series is made, no matter where the game is played, you can count on the winning team holding a wild celebration scene on the field. Players running to the diamond, the dugouts emptying, the big pile of happy players on the field—it has become one of the most joyous scenes in baseball. The Reds have had their share of championship celebrations, but oddly enough there was none in 1976. Think about it for a minute. Have you ever seen a photograph of the Reds celebrating on the Yankee Stadium infield? Reds General Manager Bob Howsam ordered the players to run off the field as fast as possible. The Yankee fans had torn up the field after New York had won its ALCS series the week before, and that was a happy crowd! Howsam worried that the Reds sweep might trigger the same kind of fan riot, and this time it would be an angry outburst. So when George Foster caught the final out, the Reds made a beeline for the clubhouse. And that's where the 1976 celebration finally broke out.

A SPUTTERING MACHINE

Turn back the clock to 1977, and the number one movie was *Annie Hall*, the number one song was "You Light Up My Life." and the number one team in baseball was the Reds, favored to win the National League pennant after their back-to-back

World Series titles. But the Big Red Machine sputtered in 1977, in part due to the trade of Tony Perez. His replacement, Dan Driessen, had a very good year offensively, but the loss of Perez's leadership seemed to take its toll—combined with some very poor pitching. Even the addition of Tom Seaver at mid-season in a blockbuster trade with the Mets could not revive the Reds. They wound up ten games behind the Dodgers in second place. But the team got some good news at season's end. George Foster, who had set a club record with fifty-two home runs, was named National League MVP.

NO HITS, FIVE RUNS

It's easy to find highlights from Joe Morgan's Hall of Fame career, but how about a night when Morgan did not have any brilliant fielding plays nor even a dramatic home run? Yet, it is a game that goes into the record books. On July 27, 1973, Joe scored four runs without a base hit. He walked four times and scored four times, which puts him second on the all-time list to...himself! On June 30, 1977, against San Francisco at Riverfront Stadium, Morgan had no hits, yet scored five runs. No one else has ever done that. He walked three times, reached once on an error, and once on a fielder's choice. He put himself in scoring position with some aggressive base running, including a couple of steals, and scored on RBI hits by Dan Driessen, George Foster, and Cesar Geronimo.

TWO-TIME MVP JOE MORGAN

VIDA BLUE TRADE

The Big Red Machine suffered a serious setback after the 1977 season. After winning two consecutive World Series, the club had traded Tony Perez and let Don Gullet leave to free agency. Even though Tom Seaver arrived in a trade, the pitching staff struggled all year. GM Bob Howsam wanted more pitching, and in the off-season he worked out a deal with the Oakland A's for Vida Blue, one of the top pitchers in the American League. But a few weeks after the deal was announced, commissioner Bowie Kuhn voided it—he thought Seaver and Blue on the same staff would create, in his words, a "competitive imbalance." But the cancellation came too late for the Reds publicity department. The 1978 media guide had already gone to the printer with Vida Blue on the team, and that is the only place where Blue appeared for the Reds.

THE HIT STREAK

On June 14, 1978, Pete Rose had two hits in a 3-1 Reds win over the Cubs at Riverfront Stadium. Nothing unusual about that for the hit king, but those knocks proved to be the start of a hitting streak that had not been seen in baseball since the days of Joe DiMaggio. The streak reached twenty-eight games on July 15 when Rose broke the modern Reds record held by Vada Pinson and Edd Roush. Now the media was alive with news of the streak, and Rose thrived in the spotlight. Each night he held court with press conferences, on the road and at home. "Fine with me," said Pete. "I like talking about my base hits." On July 25 he broke the modern NL consecutive hit record with his thirty-eighth game. He tied the all-time National League record with game number forty-four on July 31, when he knocked a single in the sixth inning off Hall of Fame pitcher Phil Niekro. The next night he was shut out. In his forty-four games, Pete collected seventy hits, and his streak improved the fiscal bottom line as well. For games forty through forty-three of the streak in Cincinnati, the Reds drew an average of forty-eight thousand—fourteen thousand over their season average. Nobody was better than Pete at putting fannies in the seats.

LAST DANCE

The number one song in 1978 was Donna Summer's *Last Dance*, which could serve as the theme song for the season; it was the last dance for manager Sparky Anderson and for Pete Rose. The winningest manager in Reds history, and one of the most beloved figures ever on the Cincinnati sports scene, was fired by Dick Wagner, club president and general manager, after the end of the 1978 season. The Reds traveled to Japan for a series of seventeen exhibition games in late October, and when the club returned, Anderson was given the news. One week later, negotiations between Rose and the Reds broke down, and Pete elected to sign as a free agent with the Phillies. You would think with all these moves the Reds were desperate, but in fact the 1978 season had hardly been a poor one. The Reds won ninety-two games and finished just two and a half games out of first. But Wagner, now in charge after Bob Howsam had resigned, wanted to put his stamp on the club, and he wound up making two of the most unpopular decisions in Reds history.

CHANGING OF THE GUARD

The 1979 season was a year of transition for the Reds, as the curtain finally closed on the Big Red Machine era. With Pete Rose signed as a free agent by the Phillies and Sparky Anderson guiding the Tigers, the familiar faces were disappearing. This year would be the last one for Joe Morgan in a Reds uniform, the last year Cesar Geronimo would be the regular center fielder. But Ray Knight filled in nicely for Rose at third, Tom Seaver and Tom Hume anchored the pitching staff, and the Reds still had enough fire power in the lineup to win the division by a game and a half over Houston. Johnny Bench reached a milestone with his 325th home run, breaking the club record held by Frank Robinson. The Reds faced the Pirates in the NLCS, and the less said about that the better; the Pirates swept the Reds on their way to winning the World Series. But one thing that still endures from 1979, and you can't avoid it at the ballpark: The Y and the M and the C and the A. Yes that was the year of the Village People's big hit, now a ballpark standard.

SPARKY ANDERSON COULD NOT BEAR TO WATCH AS THE BIG RED
MACHINE WAS DISMANTLED. HE DID NOT HAVE TO SUFFER FOR LONG.
HE WAS FIRED BY DICK WAGNER AFTER THE 1978 SEASON.

WORST TO FIRST

1980-1999

ALLEN AND O'TOOLE

The Reds, who had finished first in the NL West in 1979, were again favored to contend for the NL pennant in 1980. They had a strong pitching staff, led by Tom Seaver, Mario Soto, and Tom Hume, and an offense that featured the power of George Foster and the speed of Dave Collins. Collins, in fact, would go on to steal seventy-nine bases, just two short of the all-time club record. The Reds remained in contention until the final weeks of the season, but finished third, three and a half games behind the Astros. A couple of interesting firsts happened that year: Opening Day marked the first appearance of the famous Budweiser Clydesdale horses. They have become an annual fixture in the parade ever since. And the Reds appeared on pay television for the first time, on a short-lived subscription channel called ON-TV. The first game featured that famous Reds broadcast team of Allen and O'Toole. You do recall Allen and O'Toole, don't you? That would be Mel Allen, the famous voice of the Yankees who served as a guest announcer, and Jim O'Toole, the Reds Hall of Famer, who acted as a roving reporter.

WE STILL CAN'T BELIEVE IT

The results of the 1981 season still leave Reds fans shaking their heads. If you told someone today that at the end of this season, the Reds would have the best record in all of baseball and still not be in the playoffs, they would think you were crazy. And yet, in 1981 that is exactly what happened. Here's the story: On June 12 a players' strike interrupted the season. The Reds were in second place, one-half game behind the Dodgers. The strike dragged on for fifty days and play finally resumed on August 10.

To drum up more interest in the remaining games, the owners declared that the season would be divided into two halves. The leaders at the start of the strike would be declared the first-half winners, and they would play the winners of the second half in the playoffs. So the Reds who had finished a close second in the first half of the season to the Dodgers, had to win the second half, but instead again finished a close second, this time to the Astros, and failed to qualify. This was the first time in history that the overall season record counted for nothing. So even though their winning percentage was .611—the only team over .600 in all of baseball—the Reds season was over.

BAD LUCK MARIO

If there was ever a bad-luck pitcher for the Reds, it was the ace of the staff in the early 1980s, Mario Soto. Soto had an outstanding fastball and a devastating change of pace. From 1981 to 1985, he struck out more hitters than any pitcher in baseball. But he never won more than eighteen games. He no doubt would have had much more success if he did not have the misfortune to be at his peak when the Reds were at their worst. The club set a record for futility in 1982 with 101 losses. Soto's bad luck even wiped out his most serious bid at a no-hitter when he was stopped at the ultimate point: two strikes and two out in the ninth inning, when George Hendrick hit a home run. But his bad luck didn't keep him out of the Reds Hall of Fame. You'll find Mario Soto's plaque there the next time you visit.

HURT SO BAD

John Cougar Mellencamp had a hit with the song "Hurt So Good" in 1982, and if that truly was the case, Reds fans must have been feeling great all season. You could argue that it was one of the worst years in Reds history: a club-record 101 losses, 1.3 million in attendance, their lowest since they moved into Riverfront. The outfield of Paul Householder, Eddie Milner, and Cesar Cedeno was one of the least productive in club

MASTER OF THE CHANGE-UP, REDS ACE MARIO SOTO GAVE FANS SOMETHING TO CHEER ABOUT DURING THE BLEAK YEARS OF THE EARLY 1980S.

history, and in a truly tragic episode, the first fan fatality at a Riverfront game occurred in July when a woman committed suicide leaping from the red seats. Oddly enough, the Reds did feature two Cooperstown Hall of Famers on that squad—Johnny Bench and Tom Seaver, although both had, not surprisingly, poor years. The only bright spot came in a game that didn't count. In the 1982 All-Star Game in Montreal, Mario Soto pitched two scoreless innings, Tom Hume earned a save, and Dave Concepcion was voted the MVP by virtue of a two-run home run off Dennis Eckersly.

WHAT A GOING AWAY PARTY

The Reds had another dismal season on the field in 1983, finishing last in the Western Division for the second straight season. But off the field the news was far more

TEAMMATES PAUL HOUSEHOLDER AND NICK ESASKY CONGRATULATE JOHNNY BENCH AFTER HITTING A HOME RUN IN HIS FINAL GAME. THE HOMER WAS THE 389TH OF HIS CAREER, STILL A TEAM RECORD.

interesting. Bob Howsam returned as general manager of the Reds, replacing his former lieutenant, Dick Wagner. At the end of the season, Howsam fired manager Russ Nixon and replaced him with Vern Rapp. But the biggest news in 1983 was the announcement that Johnny Bench would retire at the end of the season. His retirement party came on September 17, an intimate little affair with over fifty thousand of his best friends filling Riverfront. And of course, Bench, who always had the ability to deliver in the clutch, didn't let the fans down. He homered on his retirement night, a line shot over the left-field wall, home run number 389, which is still the club record. And you can watch the video of Bench's final home run when you visit the Reds Hall of Fame.

PETE'S BACK!

Nineteen eighty-four was a year for famous debuts: Ronald Reagan debuted in the White House, Apple launched its MacIntosh computer with its famous Super Bowl

commercial, and *The Cosby Show* debuted on NBC. But in Cincinnati, the biggest news was a re-run: Pete Rose returned to the Reds after a five-and-a-half-year hiatus with the Phillies and the Expos. Bob Howsam, who had replaced Dick Wagner as general manager the year before, engineered the trade. Pete returned to the Reds as a player-manager, or "manager-player" as Howsam insisted he be called, because Howsam wanted to make sure Pete focused on managing first. But the fans came to see him on the diamond, and Pete did not disappoint. In his first game back on August 17, he singled in his first at-bat. When the centerfielder misplayed the ball, and with

PETE ROSE BRINGS HOPE FOR BETTER DAYS WITH HIS RETURN TO THE REDS IN 1984.

the crowd roaring with every step he took, Pete flew past second and slid head-first into third base. Rose's return had the impact Howsam wanted: Pete revived the gate, and he began to turn the team around. Under Vern Rapp, the Reds had gone 51-70; the Reds finished 19-22 under Pete. The Reds wound up fifth in 1984, but in the next four seasons under Rose the Reds became contenders, finishing second every year.

BOOM!

Reds fans hope for home runs at the ballpark, not just for the runs they score, but also for the familiar fireworks that light up the sky, and send that big boom rolling out across the river. Even fans sitting at home on their decks a few miles away from downtown can hear the fireworks, and everyone knows: another Reds home run. The tradition started in 1984 when Bob Howsam decided Riverfront Stadium needed more excitement. Howsam kept the fireworks a secret from the press and even from his own players. So when Eddie Milner homered on Opening Day, 1984, everyone, including Milner, was surprised by the rockets red glare, the bombs bursting in air. "I thought they were shooting at me," Milner said later.

A BROKEN RECORD

The Reds finished second in 1985, but Pete Rose finished first, first that is, in the all-time hit category, when on September 11, he singled to break Ty Cobb's record. Nearly fifty thousand fans filled Riverfront Stadium to watch the coronation of baseball's new hit king. But what fans may not have realized was that they were watching Pete break the hit record for the second time. When Ty Cobb retired he was credited with 4,191 hits. But scorekeeping in Cobb's era was not as rigorous as it is today, and researchers discovered that Cobb had been given two extra hits. His actual record was 4,189. But officials at Major League Baseball decided not to

PERHAPS THE MOST MEMORABLE MOMENT IN REDS HISTORY: (ABOVE) PETE ROSE
BREAKS TY COBB'S LONG-STANDING RECORD WITH HIT NUMBER 4,192. (OPPOSITE, TOP)
PETE SALUTES THE FANS AT RIVERFRONT AFTER THE HISTORIC HIT. (OPPOSITE, BELOW)
PETE HUGS HIS SON, PETE, JR., AS FANS CONTINUE THEIR OVATION.

change Cobb's original total because they feared they would be changing it frequently as other mistakes were discovered. However, no other discrepancies have been found over the years, and so it appears that Cobb's actual hit total was 4,189, which Pete broke with a single in a game in Chicago. He then broke the official record three days later in Cincinnati at Riverfront with hit 4,192. So not only did Pete break Cobb's record, but he did it twice.

PETE'S GREATEST HITS

Most Reds fans...make that most baseball fans...associate the number 4,192 with Pete and his efforts to become baseball's all-time leader in hits. But in the future, if any player threatens Pete's accomplishment, the magic number will not be 4,192; it will be 4,257. That's the total number of hits in Pete's twenty-four-year career, one that stretched over five presidential administrations from 1963 to 1986. His favorite pitcher: Phil Niekro, the Hall of Famer who gave up sixty-four knocks to Pete. Don Sutton was next on the list with sixty. And other the Hall of Famers on Pete's hit parade: Jim Bunning, Steve Carlton, Don Drysdale, Rollie Fingers, Bob Gibson, Ferguson Jenkins, Juan Marichal, Gaylord Perry, Nolan Ryan, Tom Seaver, Warren Spahn, and Hoyt Wilhelm. Pete's last hit? A single off San Francisco's Greg Minton on August 14, 1986.

TWO EPIC CAREERS

In 1986, the Reds were just four games out of first place on July 19 but lost eleven of their next fourteen to fall out of contention. With pennant dreams fading, the fans turned their attention to two of the club's greatest players, Pete Rose and Tony Perez, who were winding up their brilliant careers. They combined for forty-seven major league seasons and nearly seven thousand hits. They began their minor league careers together in 1960, debuting in Geneva, New York.

Wouldn't you like to have seen one of those games? Twenty-six seasons later, both had their final at-bats. Both came against the Padres at Riverfront Stadium. On August 17, Pete pinch hit in the bottom of the eighth inning, and facing Hall of Fame pitcher Goose Gossage, struck out. No one knew at the time that was Pete's final at-bat as he never officially announced his retirement, but it did end his twenty-four-year career. Perez, who had declared that 1986 would be his final season, homered in his next to last game, which would have been the fitting end to his twenty-three-year Hall of Fame career, but in his final game the next day, he was 0-3. Two epic baseball journeys concluded in 1986.

KNIGHT VS. DAVIS

Mention Reds Hall of Famer Eric Davis and somebody will recall his memorable bout with Ray Knight of the Mets back in 1986, a game that could be remembered for any number of reasons. A couple of controversial calls early in the game led to the ejections of Darryl Strawberry and Reds coach Billy DeMars. Then in the bottom of the ninth, with two out, and the Reds ahead, 3-1, Reds outfielder Dave Parker dropped an easy fly ball that allowed the Mets to tie the game. In extra innings, Davis slid hard into third base and tangled with Knight. That fight emptied the benches and sent four more players to the showers. The Mets wound up with no position players left and used pitchers Jesse Orosco and Roger McDowell as both outfielders and relief pitchers. McDowell was on the mound in the bottom of the fourteenth when Orosco, in left field, wound up catching the final out of the game, some five hours after the first pitch.

LARKIN VS. STILLWELL

It's easy to second guess a lot of trades, but here's one that turned out exactly right. In the mid-1980s, the Reds had two young prospects competing for the shortstop

CINCINNATI'S REDS! THE 1986 TEAM FEATURED A LOT OF HOME-GROWN TALENT. (L-R): CHRIS WELSH, DAVE PARKER, BUDDY BELL, BARRY LARKIN, RON OESTER, AND PETE ROSE

YOUNG SHORTSTOP BARRY LARKIN ATTRACTS MEDIA ATTENTION.

position: Kurt Stillwell, the Reds first-round draft choice in 1983, and Barry Larkin, a first round pick in 1985. In 1986 and 1987, Stillwell actually started more games at short than Larkin, but most of the Reds front office thought Barry had more overall talent. After the 1987 season, the Reds received several inquiries about their two shortstops, and Stillwell was the one to go, traded to Kansas City along with Ted Power for pitcher Danny Jackson. Stillwell was an All-Star that year in the American League but never again had a great year. Larkin was also chosen for the NL team in 1988, but that was just the start. Barry appeared in eleven midsummer classics, won three Gold Gloves, and an MVP award. There was no second guessing that trade.

ERIC THE GREAT

In 1987, Pete Rose managed the Reds. The team had Eric Davis, Barry Larkin, and Dave Parker in the lineup, and the Reds sailed into August in first place, led mostly by their offense. The starting pitching struggled and with an excess of outfielders, the front office was urged to trade one of them for more pitching. But that was the year of the "crown jewels." At least that is the way GM Bill Bergesch treated his outfielders. Bergesch was reluctant to part with Davis or Tracy Jones or Kal Daniels, and the Reds faded down the stretch, finishing six games behind the Giants. Despite the late-season collapse, that season had many memorable

THIRD BASEMAN BUDDY BELL CONGRATULATES SLUGGER ERIC DAVIS AFTER A
HOME RUN.

moments, and most involved Eric Davis. He hit three grand slams in May, and he stole fifty bases to go with his thirty-seven home runs. But it was his defense I recall the best, robbing Jack Clark of a home run with an over-the-fence grab and then repeating the feat against Clark the very next night! On September 4 in Chicago he made a game-saving catch with two out in the ninth, crashing into the unforgiving Wrigley Field wall. But Davis paid the price, with a rib injury that caused him to miss the next seventeen games. All in all, a highlight season for the Reds outfielder that had him compared to Willie Mays. You'll see Eric Davis's plaque when you visit the Reds Hall of Fame.

PERFECTION AND A SUSPENSION

The Reds finished second in 1988, their fourth consecutive second-place finish under manager Pete Rose. Nothing memorable about that, but 1988 had its share of other highlights. That year will be long remembered as the year of the perfect game, Tom Browning's gem on September 16. But there were plenty of other headlines made at Riverfront that year. The Reds hosted the All-Star Game in 1988, and Chris Sabo won the Rookie of the Year Award. And what about April 30 at Riverfront, when Pete Rose and umpire Dave Pallone got into a fierce argument? Pallone gestured angrily at Rose and poked him in the cheek, and Pete gave Pallone a big shove.

THE REDS ALL-STARS OF 1988 (L-R): PITCHER DANNY JACKSON, SHORTSTOP BARRY LARKIN, AND THIRD BASEMAN CHRIS SABO, WHO WOULD GO ON TO WIN THE ROOKIE OF THE YEAR AWARD.

Fans tossed debris on the field, Pallone took refuge in the umpire's dressing room, and the game resumed after a fourteen-minute delay with just three umps. Broadcasters Marty Brennaman and Joe Nuxhall received a warning from the commissioner's office for making irresponsible remarks that helped provoke the fans, and Commissioner Bart Giamatti leveled a huge fine of ten thousand dollars against Pete and suspended him for thirty days. Which, as it turned out, was not the last time those two would square off.

27 Os

The box score, that humble rectangle of statistics occupying the nooks and crannies of the morning paper. It has been a part of baseball from the beginning. You can even pick up a paper from 1869, the year of the first professional baseball team, and find box scores of the games of those original Cincinnati Red Stockings. And if you are a true box-score junkie, you know that, now, on line, you can find the box score of nearly every major league game in the last forty years. The most perfect of all box scores to me is from a no-hitter, and in Reds history, give me the box score of Tom Browning's perfect game against the Dodgers. On a rainy night at Riverfront, Browning took the mound after a two hour and twenty-seven minute rain delay. Inning after inning, he set down the Dodgers, one, two, three. His opponent wasn't too bad either. Tim Belcher had a no-hitter himself through 5 $\frac{2}{3}$ innings. But Browning was perfect all night long. All those zeroes, no hits, no walks, no runs scored, no RBIs, no errors. A perfect minimum of twenty-seven at-bats. It is the only game of its kind in the long history of the Reds. And you'll see the box score from Tom Browning's perfect night when you visit the Reds Hall of Fame.

TOM BROWNING IS EMBRACED BY TEAMMATES RON OESTER AND JEFF REED
AFTER COMPLETING HIS PERFECT GAME.

ONE MORE STRIKE

The lasting memory of that 1988 season is Tom Browning's perfect game, but he might well have had to share those honors were it not for the Expo's Wallace Johnson. For on May 2, Johnson singled with two out in the top of the ninth inning to ruin Ron Robinson's bid at a perfect game. Robinson had retired twenty-six consecutive Montreal batters and had taken the count to 2-2 against Johnson before he lined a clean hit to left field. The very next hitter, Tim Raines, hit a home run, so Robinson lost his perfect game, his no-hitter, and his shutout in just two batters. Four months later on September 16, Browning was able to get the twenty-seventh and final out for his perfect game. But the Reds came closer than any other team in history to having two perfect games in one season.

PETE STRIKES OUT

There were a lot of memorable moments for the Reds in 1989. Eric Davis hit for the cycle, the Reds scored fourteen runs in one inning against Houston, Johnny Bench was elected to the Hall of Fame in Cooperstown, and Kal Daniels and Marge Schott flipped a coin in front of live TV to settle a salary dispute (Daniels won). But the season was tainted from the beginning by the betting scandal involving Reds manager Pete Rose. The news first broke in spring training with a story in *Sports Illustrated* and the commissioner's office confirmed Pete was under investigation. While Reds game-day stories filled the sports pages, Rose stories dominated the front pages. Finally, on August 24, an agreement was reached; Rose did not admit to gambling on baseball, but he did accept a lifetime suspension from Commissioner Bart Giamatti with permission to apply for reinstatement in one year. A week later Giamatti died of a heart attack, and to this day, Rose remains on baseball's suspended list. The team, picked by many to win the Western Division in 1989, finished a miserable fifth. But good news was on the horizon: the Reds hired Lou Piniella as their new manager in November, and within a year, they were World Champs. And Pete? Convicted of tax evasion, he watched that World Series behind bars.

LIFE GOT LONELY FOR PETE ROSE IN 1989 WHEN HIS GAMBLING SCANDAL BECAME
HEADLINE NEWS, LEADING TO HIS BANISHMENT FROM THE GAME.

A PLACE FOR THE FANTASIES

As you walk down the hallway leading to the final gallery with the plaques in the Reds Hall of Fame, you will pass a large sign with the following quote: "I had no idea the Hall of Fame was waiting for me. I don't think any youngster ever thinks that's possible. Because that is a place of the fantasies." Who said it? None other than the great Johnny Bench, at his induction ceremony into Cooperstown in 1989. We asked Johnny if he might still have the notes from that speech. We wanted to display them on the wall next to the quote. But, no. They didn't exist. Turns out Johnny ad-libbed his eloquent remarks.

THE CYCLE

One of the rarest feats in baseball is for a batter to record a single, double, triple, and home run in the same game, a feat known as hitting for the cycle. You are more likely to see a triple play or watch a no-hitter. Only five Reds have hit for the cycle since 1900. Just five in one hundred and five seasons! The last Cincinnati player to accomplish the cycle was Eric Davis. It was June 2, 1989, at Riverfront Stadium against San Diego. In the first inning, Eric doubled. He singled in the third. Nothing special so far, but in the fourth, he hit a home run. Now he needed that rarest of hits, the triple, and in the seventh, he launched a long drive to deep right-center field. The fleet Davis streaked past second and slid into third base ahead of the throw, becoming the first Red to hit for the cycle since another Hall of Famer, Frank Robinson, did it in 1959. You can see the video of Davis's historic feat when you visit the Reds Hall of Fame

TWENTY BATTERS, SIXTEEN HITS, FOURTEEN RUNS, ONE INNING

On August 3, 1989, Ken Griffey, Sr., the Reds left fielder, had a good day, with two hits, including a home run and four RBIs—and that was just in the first inning! On that date, against the Astros at Riverfront Stadium, the Reds scored fourteen runs in the first, the most the club ever scored in one inning. The team also set club records for most hits in one inning with sixteen and most singles in one inning with twelve. Twenty batters went to the plate; Mariano Duncan and Luis Quinones each batted three times. Here's the way the hitting marathon unfolded: walk, bunt, single, single, home run, three more singles, a double, a ground out by pitcher Tom Browning, another double, four more singles, another double, then three more singles, and mercifully, two fly outs to end the inning. With the bases still loaded! As catcher Jeff Reed put it, "Everybody was up to the plate swinging because everything fell in. Everybody was trying to grab bats at once!"

WIRE-TO-WIRE-TO-SWEEP

After the miserable 1989 season, marred by the Rose suspension and the fifth-place finish, no one knew what to expect for 1990. The scandal prompted owner Marge Schott to make wholesale changes in her operation, and it turned out she made some very good moves. She brought in a new manager, Lou Piniella, and a new general manager, Bob Quinn. Piniella took one look at his club in spring training, and told them, "You're too good not to have won anything." Now, it's never as simple as teams turning things around after just one comment, but Piniella did set a tone that the Reds responded to eagerly. They won their first nine games in a row—the best start in team history. They jumped out to a 30-12 record by the end of May. And as it turned out, the season was over. The Reds led every day and that earned the team its first nickname: The Wire-to-Wire Champs. However, they struggled down the stretch and faced the Pirates who had a better season record. But the Reds took the NLCS, four games to two and then faced the mighty Oakland A's in the World Series. Heavy underdogs, the Reds won the first game behind Eric Davis's first-inning home run, then won the second on Joe Oliver's tenth-inning single. They won Game Three on the strength of a seven-run third inning, and then Jose Rijo beat the A's in Game Four. And that stunning four-game victory led to the other enduring nickname from that season: "Sweep!"

THE REDS CELEBRATE THEIR SWEEP OF THE OAKLAND A'S TO WIN THE WORLD SERIES
ON OCTOBER, 20, 1990.

NASTY BOYS

In 1988, two young pitchers made their debuts with the Reds: fireballer Rob Dibble and Norm Charlton. Both were used mainly in relief, and in 1990, they were joined by closer Randy Myers, who the Reds picked up in a trade for John Franco. The three bullpen aces quickly proved to be a dominating weapon for manager Lou Piniella. Game after game, Dibble and Charlton came in to set up Myers for the save. The threesome soon began calling themselves the Nasty Boys, a nickname they picked up from a short-lived television series about a police unit in Las Vegas. The trio came to personalize that 1990 championship squad: swaggering

THE NASTY BOYS: RANDY MYERS, ROB DIBBLE, AND NORM CHARLTON

and confident and very, very good. They combined for forty-four saves, and, as Piniella later said, the Nasty Boys made it a six-inning game. For if the Reds were ahead by the sixth and needed help from the bullpen, the Nasty Boys knew how to close the door. In games the Reds led after six innings, their record was 70-6. Now that's a bullpen.

BATES AND BRAGGS

Houston has had the "Killer B's" in recent years, the duo of Jeff Bagwell and Craig Biggio [And Lance Berkman?]. But in 1990, the Reds had their version of the Killer B's in the post-season: Glenn Braggs and Billy Bates. Braggs and Bates joined the Reds in June after a trade with the Brewers and both were bench players. But during the playoffs and the World Series, they were each responsible for a spine-tingling moment that helped the Reds win a championship. Braggs leaped high against the right-field wall in the ninth inning of the final game of the playoffs to rob Carmelo Martinez of a home run and preserve the Reds 2-1 victory over the Pirates. In Game Two of the World Series, Bates came off the bench to ignite a tenth-inning rally with an infield single. He scored the winning run moments later on a Joe Oliver single.

FELLOW POST-SEASON HERO GLENN BRAGGS CONGRATULATES BILLY BATES, WHO HAS JUST SCORED THE WINNING RUN IN GAME TWO OF THE 1990 WORLD SERIES.

LOU THROWS OUT FIRST

Ask Reds fans about Lou Piniella, and they recall the former manager with great fondness, not only for leading the club to the 1990 World Championship but also for one memorable night at Riverfront when he engaged in a furious argument with umpire Dutch Rennert. Piniella stormed out of the dugout when Rennert called Barry Larkin out at first. Lou pulled first base out of the ground and threw it toward right field—not once but twice, as the fans went crazy. The historic toss was measured at thirty-five feet, and two days later, at Fountain Square, the *Cincinnati Enquirer* sponsored a base-tossing contest in honor of Lou's record heave. You can watch Lou's performance when you visit the Reds Hall of Fame.

ONE OF THE MOST FAMOUS THROWS IN TEAM HISTORY: MANAGER LOU PINELLA TOSSES FIRST BASE TOWARD RIGHT FIELD TO PROTEST AN UMPIRE'S CALL.

THAT BALL IS OUTTA HERE!

"Achy Breaky Heart" was the number one song in 1991, and the Reds broke a few hearts that year as well. Cincinnati was the defending World Champions, most of the key players were back, and talk of dynasty was in the air. But there was no repeat of the wire-to-wire thrills of 1990. A ton of injuries in the second half of the season ended any hopes of a repeat, and the Reds fell below .500 and finished fifth. Whatever headlines the Reds garnered that season seemed to belong to Rob

Dibble, one of the three Nasty Boys. But the headlines weren't positive: Dibble's temper got the best of him on several occasions, including one night at Riverfront when he struggled to get a save. He finally recorded the last out, took the ball and, in frustration, launched it toward center field, where, soaring some four hundred feet like a well-struck home run, it cleared the fence and landed in the green seats, hitting a surprised fan. Dibble was suspended four games, and he paid for the fan's medical expenses.

GRIFFEY, SR. AND MORRIS

The last Red to win a batting title was Pete Rose in 1973. Since then the two Reds with the best chance to win the title were Ken Griffey, Sr. and Hal Morris, and both were in contention until the final day of the season. Griffey came within a whisker in 1976, losing to Bill Madlock of the Cubs, when Madlock went 4-for-4. In 1991, Terry Pendleton of Atlanta had a .319 average on the final day and sat out the last game. Morris needed a 4-for-4 or 4-for-5 day to win the crown. And he was on his way. He singled in his first three at-bats. On his fourth trip to the plate, he lined out. Now, he needed just one more opportunity. But the game ended with Morris in the on-deck circle, and he finished just one percentage point behind Pendleton.

A FINAL HOME RUN SWING

After a disappointing year in 1991, the Reds under manager Lou Piniella started the 1992 season in contention, and on July 7 they enjoyed a six-game lead in the Western Division pennant race. But over the next three weeks, the Reds lost every bit of that lead, and although they went on to win ninety games, they finished second, eight games behind the Braves. It was to be Piniella's last year as manager of the Reds. It was also the last year for Glenn Braggs in a Reds uniform. One of the stars of the 1990 World Series team, Braggs ended his major league career in 1992 with one of the most unusual injuries in baseball history. He tore cartilage in his knee…during a home run trot! After hitting a homer against the Braves, he took three or four steps and came up lame. It took him almost two minutes to make the tour of the bases. That was his final major league at bat, at the age of twenty-nine.

TEN STRAIGHT HITS

You might think the club record for most consecutive hits would belong to the hit king, Pete Rose. But the club record actually belongs to Bip Roberts and a shortstop

from the 1940s named Woody Williams. Roberts tied Williams's mark in 1992 over four games. He had hits in his last two at bats in the first game, then went 4-for-4 and 3-for-3 to reach nine consecutive hits. In LA, Roberts faced Pedro Astacio and singled in his first at-bat to record ten hits in a row. That not only tied Roberts for the Reds record, it also tied him for the National League record. Needing one more hit to set the all-time mark, he grounded out. His streak ended with six singles and four doubles, an amazing stretch of hitting.

**THE CONSECUTIVE HIT KING:
BIP ROBERTS**

DISHWASHERS AND ROOFTOPS

About the only thing that wasn't memorable about the 1993 season was the Reds finish. They wound up a mediocre fourth, thirty-one games behind the Braves. But

TONY PEREZ'S TENURE AS
REDS MANAGER LASTED ONLY
FORTY-FOUR GAMES.

during the course of that season, what a smorgasbord of memories. There was the good: the Cardinals' Mark Whiten hit four consecutive home runs at Riverfront to tie the major league record. There was the bad: the firing of Tony Perez after only forty-four games. There was the ugly: owner Marge Schott was suspended for one year for making racial and ethnic slurs. And then there was the just plain wacky. Hal Morris injured his shoulder during a brawl…in spring training! Joe Oliver missed three games when he cut his finger, unloading his dishwasher! And, Tom Browning was fined after making an impromptu visit to the rooftop of a building facing Wrigley Field. This probably would not have landed Browning in quite so much trouble had he not done it during a game, and in uniform! But maybe it brought the team some good luck. While Browning was there, Kevin Mitchell hit a home run, and the Reds won the game, 4-3. But the seat was expensive. Tom paid a fine of one thousand dollars.

MARK WHITEN'S FOUR HOME RUNS

The major league record for most home runs in one game is four, and no Red has ever accomplished that. But it happened once by a Reds opponent, Mark Whiten of the St. Louis Cardinals. In the second game of a doubleheader on September 7, 1993, at Riverfront, Whiten not only hit four homers but also knocked in twelve runs. Both feats tied major league records. His first home run was a grand slam, the second and third homers each came with two on, and his final blast was a two-run homer. His first pitching victim was Larry Leubers, who gave up the grand slam. The next two came off Mike Anderson (whose big league career only lasted three games), and Whiten hit the final blast off Rob Dibble.

TWO OPENERS

Opening Day is so big in Cincinnati that in 1994 we had not one, but two openers! In 1994, Major League Baseball and ESPN decided, in a salute to Reds history, to start the season with the first game in Cincinnati, a tradition the Reds had enjoyed for most of the 1950s, 60s and 70s. But the honor came with a price. The opener was scheduled for Sunday night, which did not sit well with owner Marge Schott. It was a weekend date, Easter Sunday of all things, and it was a night game. Openers in Cincinnati had always been held on weekdays, during the daytime, and Mrs. Schott decided to downplay the Sunday night opener, and instead she put out the word that the Reds would be honoring the second game of the season, on Monday afternoon, as the "real opener." So into Cincinnati comes ESPN and the start of the baseball

OWNER MARGE SCHOTT WITH HER BELOVED SAINT BERNARDS

season, and they are greeted by the deafening sound of...silence. No bunting, no parade, no elaborate pre-game ceremonies. And only thirty-two thousand fans, far less than the typical full house. Instead, the Reds celebrated their traditional Opening Day, the next day on Monday, with all the traditional festivities. That ESPN Sunday night "opener" counted in the official standings, but not in the hearts of Reds fans.

KEVIN MITCHELL AND HAL MORRIS LED THE NUMBER ONE OFFENSE IN THE
NATIONAL LEAGUE IN STRIKE-SHORTENED 1994.

ONE STRIKE AND YOU'RE OUT

If you were writing the history of baseball a few years ago, you might have wondered if 1994 would go down in history as the year that killed the game. For 1994 was the year the season ended early, and the World Series was canceled. On August 12, the players went on strike after the two sides could not reach agreement on a new contract, and as it turned out the Reds were the big losers. They had the number one offense in the league at that point, led by Kevin Mitchell, Hal Morris, and Barry Larkin. Their pitching—led by Jose Rijo, John Smiley, and closer Jeff Brantley—was ranked third. The Reds appeared to be a lock for the playoffs once play resumed, but then came the stunning news. On September 7 the owners voted twenty-eight to two not to resume the season and to cancel the post-season. The two "no" votes were cast by Peter Angelos, owner of the Baltimore Orioles, and by the owner of the Reds, Marge Schott. The fallout from the strike and the cancellation of the series was felt throughout baseball, especially here in Cincinnati. The Reds were on pace to draw well over two million fans in 1994, but with fans angry about the cancelled season, the Reds didn't hit that mark again until 1999.

NO REPLACEMENTS

Spring time, and the thoughts of baseball fans everywhere turned to spring training, the start of the season, and...replacement players! Remember those? The strike that had wiped out the end of the 1994 season was still going on as the 1995 season began. The owners were determined to start the season on time and began signing second-rate players to replace their regular lineups. The Reds even signed forty-eight-year-old Pedro Borbon, who was last seen pitching back in the era of the Big Red Machine. But finally on the eve of the opener, the long strike was settled, the regular players reported to camp, and the season began three weeks late on April 26. The Reds started slowly, but beginning on May 6, the club played nearly .700 ball until the end of August and ran away with the division title. The Reds swept the Dodgers in the NL Division Series, but then fell victim to the Braves' outstanding pitching in the NLCS, scoring only five runs in four games, and were swept four games to none. Barry Larkin ran away with the National League MVP award, the first Reds winner since George Foster in 1977, and Pete Schourek finished second in the Cy Young Award, the best finish by a Reds pitcher since Danny Jackson finished second in 1988.

ALL SHOOK UP

The Reds were off to a slow start in 1996 and spent most of May in last place. But in early June, the players finally discovered why. Of course, it was the bust of Elvis in the radio booth! A faithful listener to Marty and Joe had sent them a statue of the King, and the broadcasters gave it a prominent place in the booth, where it could be clearly seen by the fans and the players. It became quite a conversation piece, but apparently Elvis was sending off vibes that somehow affected the team. All shook up, the players asked Marty to send Elvis out of the building, claiming the King was bad luck. Elvis departed, but as Marty said, "If they have to blame the radio booth for their worst start in many years, that's pretty weak." Actually, maybe the players knew something. Without the King looking down, they played winning ball the rest of the season and finished at .500, in third place.

A TRAGIC OPENER

A bright sunny day at Riverfront greeted the traditional sold-out crowd for the opening of the 1996 baseball season, with pre-game ceremonies highlighted by the appearance of Sparky Anderson as the grand marshal of the Findlay Market parade. But then—tragedy. Just seven pitches into the game, home plate umpire John McSherry motioned for help, turned and began walking toward the screen behind home plate and suddenly collapsed. Medical staff from both dugouts immediately rushed to help the big umpire. After several silent moments, with the sold-out crowd standing in shock, McSherry was placed on a stretcher and taken to the hospital. He was pronounced dead of a heart attack fifty-four minutes later. After some confusion about continuing the game, the players from both teams, the Reds and the Expos, agreed they could not play. The game was postponed until the next day, when in a very subdued opener, the Reds defeated the Expos, 4-1. McSherry's

**UMPIRE JERRY CRAWFORD IN A MOMENT OF REFLECTION THE DAY FOLLOWING
JOHN McSHERRY'S SUDDEN COLLAPSE DURING THE 1996 SEASON OPENER.**

death was only the second on-field incident in a major league game. Baseball's other on-field tragedy was the beaning of Cleveland's Ray Chapman in 1920 that resulted in Chapman's death.

FOUR HOME RUNS IN ONE INNING

Twice in Reds history, the club has hit four home runs in one inning. And two of the four players contributed to both record performances. The first four-homer inning was on June 19, 1994, at Atlanta when the Reds connected off likely Hall of Famer John Smoltz in the first inning. The home runs came off the bats of Hal Morris, Kevin Mitchell, Jeff Branson, and Eddie Taubensee. Two years later, on August 17, 1996, at home against the Rockies, the Reds again launched four blasts in one inning. This time the hitters included Reggie Sanders, Barry Larkin, and reprising their slugging roles, were Branson and Taubensee. Interestingly, the four home runs in one inning is not the major league record. The record is five, and it has been done three times: in 1939 by the Giants, in 1949 by the Phillies, and in 1961 again by the Giants...and every time it was against the Reds. Now, if we could just figure out how to hit off our own pitching!

THE POWER OF WHISKERS

You knew it wouldn't be business as usual when, early in the spring of 1999, owner Marge Schott lifted the club's thirty-year ban on facial hair, and Greg Vaughn and Dimitri Young took advantage with goatees, even if Young's was dyed day-glo yellow. Or was it orange? Then came another bombshell, the announcement that the beleaguered Schott was selling the club to Cincinnati business leader and philanthropist Carl Lindner. The combination of new ownership and whiskers proved powerful. The Reds pulled off some memorable come-back victories and put up a football-like score on May 19 at Coors Field when they scored

GREG VAUGHN'S GOATEE ENDS A LONG-STANDING REDS TRADITION PROHIBITING FACIAL HAIR.

twenty-four runs, setting a slew of club records. They tied another record on August 21 with two grand slams in the same game, when Aaron Boone and Eddie Taubensee connected, and they set an NL record with nine home runs in one game against the Phillies. All this offense helped propel the team to ninety-six victories and a tie with the Mets for the Wild Card berth. But they had run out of power. The Mets, behind Al Leiter, shut out the Reds, 5-0, in the one-game playoff at Cinergy Field, and the Reds failed to qualify for the playoffs.

DOWN TO THE WIRE

The 1999 finish was one of the closest in Reds history. It would be nice to recap all the division titles or pennant titles the Reds have won on the final day of the season, but the fact is the Reds have never clinched the division or won a pennant in their final game of the regular season. The closest they came was in 1979 when they clinched the Western Division with just two games left and wound up winning the division over the Astros by one and a half games. The biggest runaway was in 1975 when the Reds had a twenty-game lead in early September and clinched on September 7, the earliest clinching date for a pennant or a division win in National League history. On the bad news front, twice in club history the Reds have lost a bid for post-season play on the final game of the season: Once in 1964, and in 1999, when the Reds lost the one-game playoff with the Mets.

THE 1999 HOME RUN GANG: FRONT ROW (L-R):
EDDIE TAUBENSEE, POKEY REESE, JEFFREY HAMMONDS
SECOND ROW (L-R): AARON BOONE, MARK LEWIS, BRIAN JOHNSON,
GREG VAUGHN, DMITRI YOUNG

BOMBS AWAY

In Reds history, the 1956 club is revered for its raw power and home run slugging. But the 1999 Reds should also be remembered when it comes to home runs. They set club records, most of them coming in an early September stretch that saw them hit twenty-one home runs in five straight games, tying the major league record. The club launched the binge on September 4 when the Reds set a National League record by hitting nine home runs in one game, in a 22-3 drubbing of the Phillies at Veterans Stadium. The nine home runs were hit by eight different players, which set a major league record. The home run bashers were Dimitri Young, Jeffrey Hammonds, Greg Vaughn, Aaron Boone, Pokey Reese, Mark Lewis, Brian Johnson, and the only man to hit two that day: Eddie Taubensee.

REDS HALL OF FAMER JOHNNY BENCH IS FLANKED BY TOM NEYER, CRAIG LINDNER, CARL LINDNER, BUD SELIG AND BOB TAFT AT THE 2000 GROUNDBREAKING FOR GREAT AMERICAN BALL PARK.

NEW MILLENIUM,
NEW BALLPARK

2000-

A FOURSOME IN COOPERSTOWN

The millennium dawned on January 1, 2000, but for Reds fans the new era began six weeks later on February 10, when Ken Griffey, Jr. joined the Reds after a trade with Seattle. With the exception of Pete Rose's return to Cincinnati in 1984, never has a player come to the Reds with more fanfare. Junior signed a nine-year contract with Cincinnati, the biggest free-agent signing in club history, and it brought one of the greatest players of all time to the Reds.

KEN GRIFFEY, JR., WITH REDS OWNER CARL LINDNER AT THE ANNOUNCEMENT PRESS CONFERENCE IN 2000

With the addition of Griffey to a team that had missed the playoffs by just one game the year before, Reds fans had high hopes heading into the 2000 season. Griffey did his part with forty home runs and 118 RBIs. But the Reds wound up second, ten games behind St. Louis. One highlight for Reds fans in 2000 happened in a quiet little village in upstate New York...in Cooperstown, when Tony Perez, Sparky Anderson, Bid McPhee, and Marty Brennaman were all honored in Hall of Fame ceremonies.

SPARKY

No manager in the history of the Reds has been more beloved than George "Sparky" Anderson, the skipper of the Big Red Machine. Anderson was elected to the National Baseball Hall of Fame and to the Reds Hall of Fame in 2000, and his number ten was retired by the Reds in 2005. Sparky became only the fifth Red to enjoy all three of these prestigious honors. Memories of Sparky abound, but do you recall how he always kept his hands in his back pockets when he went out to argue a play? That habit started in the minors after Sparky shoved an umpire. Fearing he would be kicked out baseball, Sparky vowed never to let that happen again, and from that time on, his hands stayed in his back pockets on his visits to see the men in blue. You can pose with a statue of the "Main Spark" when you visit the Reds Hall of Fame.

CURTAIN FALLS

Cincinnati jumped off to a great start in 2002, spending fifty-seven days in first place, but they lost eight in a row in mid-June and never recovered, winding up third in the division, nineteen games behind the Cardinals. But despite the losing season, 2002 will be fondly remembered as the final year of Cinergy Field, and of course, before that, it was known as Riverfront Stadium, the home of the Big Red

Machine and the 1990 World Champs. In thirty-three seasons, the Reds played 2576 regular season games before over sixty-four-million fans at the historic ballpark. As Crosley Field was to a generation before, Riverfront was the home of the Reds and thousands and thousands of fans saw their first games there, rooted for Pete Rose and Johnny Bench and Tony Perez and Dave Concepcion and Barry Larkin. What was your memorable moment at Riverfront? Something from the Big Red Machine era? The 1970 All-Star Game? The 1975 and 1976 World Series? How about Game Two of the 1990 World Series and Joe Oliver's game-winning hit? My personal favorite: Game Five of the 1972 playoffs with George Foster scoring the pennant-clinching run on a wild pitch. A full house came to say goodbye in the finale on September 22, 2002, and watched the Reds lose to the Phillies, 4-3, but Reds fans knew they had a winner in Riverfront Stadium.

Cincinnati Reds

CINERGY FIELD (NÉ RIVERFRONT STADIUM) GOES BOOM.

FROM ST. LOUIS TO THE OHIO

The Reds spent thirty-two days in first place in 2004, thanks to a strong start, and they went into June with a two-game lead in the NL Central. But the wheels fell off starting in early June. The Reds suffered a seven-game losing streak and never regained the lead, finishing in fourth place. The season is perhaps best remembered for some milestone moments: in St. Louis, Ken Griffey, Jr. walloped his five hundredth home run on Father's Day (in front of his dad, Ken Griffey, Sr.), Joe Nuxhall completed his last year as a full-time broadcaster, Steve Stewart joined the Reds announcing team, the Reds dedicated the statue of Ernie Lombardi in front of the ballpark on Crosley Terrace, the Reds honored their late owner Marge Schott, who passed away in March, with a moment of silence on Opening Day, and Adam Dunn thrilled a Great American crowd when his titanic blast on August 10 sailed far over the centerfield fence and wound up on a piece of driftwood on the Public Landing on the banks of the Ohio River. And in September of 2004, the Reds christened their new Hall of Fame, where you will can see video of Griffey's historic home run and other memorable highlights from Reds history on display all year round.

HOMERVILLE

The 2005 season saw the Reds falter early, and despite playing over .500 ball in the second half of the year, the club wound up in fifth place, suffering a fifth straight losing season, their worst stretch of sub-.500 baseball since the early 1950s. Great American Ball Park, in its third season, continued to be a home run paradise. The Reds hit 126 round-trippers at home and only ninety-six on the road. Overall, 246 balls sailed out of the park in 2005, making Great American "Small" Park, as *Cincinnati Enquirer* columnist Paul Daugherty called it, the best home run park in the major leagues that year. Since it opened, there have been an average of over two home runs per game. No wonder there were a lot of smiles at the ballpark in early June when the Baltimore Orioles visited Cincinnati. The

lineups of the two clubs included not one, not two, but three members of the five hundred home run club: Ken Griffey, Jr., Sammy Sosa, and Rafael Palmeiro. This was the first time in baseball history that three members of that home run club appeared in the same game. And no, all three didn't homer, but on June 12 Sosa and Griffey did hit long balls, which was just the fourth time in history that two members of the elite club hit one in the same game.

SHADES OF DERRINGER AND WALTERS?

Cincinnati Reds

BRONSON ARROYO

The 2006 Reds remained in contention until the final week of the season, despite an 80-82 record. When the first place team in your division only wins eighty-three games, even an eighty-win season stands a chance. In fact, the Reds were not eliminated from post-season play until the second-to-last day of the season. The other story of 2006 was (surprisingly for long-suffering fans of Reds pitching) the Reds starters, particularly Aaron Harang and Bronson Arroyo. It's a little too early to start comparing them to the best one-two punch ever in Reds history—Paul Derringer and Bucky Walters of the 1939-1940 championship teams—but Harang and Arroyo

Cincinnati Reds

AARON HARANG

have created a buzz about Reds starters that fans haven't heard for a while. The two threw nine complete games, which led the NL, the first time the Reds led the league in that category since 1944! Sixty-two years! Of course, those 1944 Reds had ninety-three complete games, but that was a very different era. Harang led the league in strikeouts, the first Reds pitcher to do that since Jose Rijo in 1993. And fans who are used to seeing the Reds near the bottom in ERA instead found them seventh in the NL, which was certainly respectable. And all of these feats were accomplished in a ballpark that is widely considered to be a hitter's park.

RELIVE MANY OF THE GREAT MOMENTS
YOU'VE READ ABOUT WHEN YOU VISIT THE

LOCATED ON THE WEST SIDE OF GREAT AMERICAN BALL PARK
ALONG MAIN STREET.

CINCINNATI REDS HALL OF FAME MEMBERS

WITH YEAR OF INDUCTION

PAUL DERRINGER (1958)

ERNIE LOMBARDI (1958)

FRANK McCORMICK (1958)

JOHNNY VANDER MEER (1958)

BUCKY WALTERS (1958)

IVAL GOODMAN (1959)

EPPA RIXEY (1959)

EWELL BLACKWELL (1960)

EDD ROUSH (1960)

LONNY FREY (1961)

BILLY WERBER (1961)

HUGHIE CRITZ (1962)

BUBBLES HARGRAVE (1962)

TED KLUSZEWSKI (1962)

RUBE BRESSLER (1963)

HARRY CRAFT (1963)

HEINIE GROH (1963)

NOODLES HAHN (1963)

GUS BELL (1964)

PETE DONOHUE (1964)

FRED HUTCHINSON (1965)

LARRY KOPF (1965)

RED LUCAS (1965)

WALLY POST (1965)

JOHNNY TEMPLE (1965)

JAKE DAUBERT (1966)

MIKE McCORMICK (1966)

BILLY MYERS (1966)

DOLF LUQUE (1967)

BILL McKECHNIE (1967)

SAM CRAWFORD (1968)

JOE NUXHALL (1968)

WARREN C. GILES (1969)

JIM O'TOOLE (1970)

ROY McMILLAN (1971)

GORDY COLEMAN (1972)

JIM MALONEY (1973)

BOB PURKEY (1974)

SMOKY BURGESS (1975)

BROOKS LAWRENCE (1976)

VADA PINSON (1977)

FRANK ROBINSON (1978)

TOMMY HELMS (1979)

CLAY CARROLL (1980)

LEO CARDENAS (1981)

WAYNE GRANGER (1982)

GARY NOLAN (1983)

JACK BILLINGHAM (1984)

JOHNNY BENCH (1986)

JOE MORGAN (1987)

JERRY LYNCH (1988)

TONY PEREZ (1988)

ED (CY) SEYMOUR (1988)

SPARKY ANDERSON (2000)

DAVE CONCEPCION (2000)

BOB EWING (2001)

MARIO SOTO (2001)

BID McPHEE (2002)

DON GULLETT (2002)

GEORGE FOSTER (2003)

DUMMY HOY (2003)

KEN GRIFFEY SR. (2004)

BOB HOWSAM (2004)

WILL WHITE (2004)

ERIC DAVIS (2005)

JOSE RIJO (2005)

HARRY WRIGHT (2005)

GEORGE WRIGHT (2005)

TOM BROWNING (2006)

LEE MAY (2006)

TOM SEAVER (2006)

ABOUT THE AUTHOR

GREG RHODES is the Executive Director of the Cincinnati Reds Hall of Fame and Museum and Cincinnati Reds Team Historian. This is his seventh book about the Cincinnati Reds, including *Redleg Journal* and *Reds in Black and White*, both winners of The Sporting News-SABR Baseball Research Award. Rhodes lives in Cincinnati with his wife, Sallie Westheimer.

REDS ON RADIO NETWORK COORDINATOR DAVE ARMBRUSTER,
NETWORK PRODUCER RUSS JACKSON, AND AUTHOR GREG RHODES
AT THE 700 WLW STUDIOS